Lectures against Sociolinguistics

PETER LANG
New York • Washington, D.C./Baltimore
Bern • Frankfurt am Main • Berlin • Vienna • Paris

Rajendra Singh

Lectures against Sociolinguistics

PETER LANG
New York • Washington, D.C./Baltimore
Bern • Frankfurt am Main • Berlin • Vienna • Paris

Library of Congress Cataloging-in-Publication Data

Singh, Rajendra.
Lectures against sociolinguistics/ Rajendra Singh.
p. cm.
Includes bibliographical references (p.) and index.
1. Sociolinguistics—Methodology. I. Title.
P40.S464 306.4'4—dc20 95-49572
ISBN 0-8204-3097-8

Die Deutsche Bibliothek-CIP-Einheitsaufnahme

Singh, Rajendra:
Lectures against sociolinguistics/ Rajendra Singh.
–New York; Washington, D.C./Baltimore; Bern; Frankfurt am Main;
Berlin; Vienna; Paris: Lang.
ISBN 0-8204-3097-8

Cover design by James F. Brisson.

For

Étienne, Jayant, Patrick, Vijay, and Vinod,

friends with whose help I have gotten by.

I shall not attempt to be conciliatory, both because I think the new philosophy ... is critically different from traditional philosophy, and because I think it is worth trying to bring out their differences as fully as possible.

—S. Cavell 1964 [1958]: 76

ACKNOWLEDGEMENTS

I am grateful to the following publishers for permission to freely use the papers and articles mentioned against their names:

Cambridge University Press: R. Singh and J. K. Lele, 1990, "Language, Power and Cross-Sex Communication Strategies in Hindi and Indian English Revisited", *Language in Society* 19, 541-546; R. Singh *et al*., 1988, "Communication in a Multilingual Society: Some Missed Opportunities", *Language and Society* 17, 43-59.

Elsevier Science, Amsterdam: J. K. Lele and R. Singh, 1991, "And Never the Twain Shall Meet or Language and Politics *chez* Chomsky: A Review of Noam Chomsky's *Language and Problems of Knowledge* and *On Power and Ideology*", *Journal of Pragmatics* 15, 175-194.

Sage Publications, New-Delhi: R. Singh and J. K. Lele, 1995, "The Autonomy of Social Variables: The Indian Evidence Revisited", in R. Singh *et al*., eds., *Explorations in Indian Sociolinguistics*, 60-81.

The audio-record of most of the lectures that make up this book was kept by Sunadi, the NUS Phonetics Laboratory maestro. The tapes were transcribed, as labor of love, by my wife. The transcriptions were typed by Fatimah Ahmad. Considerable moral support was provided by Drs. L. Onederra, Anne Pakir, N.S. Prabhu and Jean D'Souza, who kept listening even when there was *primia facie* reason to suspect. Without the help of these individuals, my sustained protests against the dominant ways of doing sociolinguistics would have never reached such a volume. I am grateful to them. I am also grateful to Alan Ford, Y.-C. Morin, and John Reighard for helping me make those protests better than they might have been without their helpful suggestions; to Jean-François Couturier and Richard Desrochers for their kind technological and moral support throughout the preparation of this manuscript.

Last but not least, I am also grateful to my sociolinguistic co-authors for their permission to use as mine what might originally have been theirs.

CONTENTS

FOREWORD

My credentials for writing this foreword are not that I am a specialist on the topics dealt with in these lectures, but rather that I had the privilege of listening to most of them when they were given at the National University of Singapore. I found those lectures both enjoyable as carefully-crafted, elegantly worded arguments, and thought-provoking as a highly-independent conception of language in society, clearly the result of many years of reflection and a steady pursuit of understanding, often at the expense of popularity. Although I did not have the opportunity to hear the three additional lectures included in this volume, they are every bit as elegant and thought-provoking as the ones I did hear. Since the artistry of exposition is better experienced than talked about, I shall limit what I say to the conception of sociolinguistics, as I saw it, and to some of the thoughts it provoked.

Singh conceives of human linguisticality and people's knowledge of particular languages somewhat differently from the way universal grammar and the grammars of particular languages are thought of in present-day generative linguistics. First, human linguisticality is for him a language-MAKING capacity, the capacity from which all natural languages arose and changed in the past and will arise and change in the future. It is constrained in specific ways, just as universal grammar is, but its cons-traints are not necessarily defined by the minimum freedom needed by the grammars of all known languages, as the constraints of universal grammar are taken to be. The constraints of linguisticality should also allow for the freedom which lies behind language change, language innovation, verbal irony and humour, creolization and all language learners' errors, since none of these phenomena can reasonably be said to transgress the linguistic laws of human nature. Human linguisticality, that is to say, may well exceed its factual manifestation in all known languages; and there is no need for any assumption than what is found in such MARGINAL phenomena as language innovation and learners' errors is less legitimate evidence of that capacity that what is found in the LAWFUL grammar of a natural language. Only the grammars of particular languages, operating as shared linguistic systems in speech communities, with the degree of sharing providing a measure of LAWFULNESS, can have use for a distinction between LAWFUL and MARGINAL phenomena; human linguisticality as such can have no use for it.

Secondly, the grammar of a particular language is for Singh not just a manifestation of human linguisticality. It is the outcome of an interaction between two human attributes — linguisticality and sociality. In the shared system of a speech community, the system is an expression of linguisticality, while the sharing is an expression of sociality. Individual linguistic creativity is curbed by the social constraints of sharing, thus promoting conformity and stability; but individual creativity can also bring about instability and change in the shared system, through non-conformity. Similarly, the tendencies of sociality, in forms such as group identity, social aspiration, the emergence of, and resistance to, elites, the distribution and negotiation of power between sections, etc., exert an influence on the shared system, causing degrees of divergence or convergence in it, creating conditions of stability or instability, and perhaps producing a measure of linguistic stratification as a reflection of social stratification. All such effects of sociality on the shared system, however, are still subject to the inherent constraints of linguisticality. In this sense, the workings of a shared system in a speech community (i.e. of a LANGUAGE) are continually held in tension by the dual forces of human linguisticality and sociality, and sociolinguistics is, in essence, a study of those workings, hazily understood at present. No sociolinguistic enquiry can therefore hope to be productive if it leaves out of consideration either of the two basic forces.

Given this perspective on what sociolinguistics is or ought to be about, it is not difficult to see why Singh is fiercely critical of several current lines of enquiry which go under that label. He is critical of some lines of work because they leave the inherent constraint and creativity of human linguisticality entirely out of account. Statistical studies of language variation, for instance, apparently assume that language is free to vary indefinitely according to contextual factors. Researchers in contact-induced language change and code-mixing also speak of their findings as if the social and contextual factors identified were solely responsible for the linguistic effects, with no general constraint from linguisticality. Indeed, such studies take some trouble to deny themselves any recourse to the constraints of linguisticality, by adopting an anti-generative stance and claiming to be alternative accounts of the nature of human language. The price they pay for this stance is to impoverish the very object of their enquiry. If there are no general constraints on possible language variation, there can be no genuine creativity, either: given certain social factors, certain language forms must follow, to the degree of probability discovered by variation studies. Language use in a human society must then be a matter of different individuals replicating given statistical correlatives between their social contexts and the forms of language. To realise how impoverished a view this is of language in society, one only has to ask what robotists might have to do to make their robots speak naturally: they will just have to feed into the robots sets of language forms and contextual factors, and the precise correlations between the two. Robot behaviour is entirely REGULATIVE, as Singh uses the term.

Singh is critical of certain other lines of work because, while not necessarily denying human linguisticality, they tend to assume or imply that linguisticality can be differentially distributed between different classes of humans. Many cross-cultural communication studies project differential language proficiency as a difference in culture-based discourse strategies, and then equate culture with ethnicity, thus implying that different ethnic groups can be endowed with different measures of linguisticality or sociality. Similarly, much discussion of NON-NATIVE varieties of English exploits a historical fact (namely, that speakers of NON-NATIVE varieties were once learners of a NATIVE variety) to assume that there are permanent, qualitative differencies between NATIVE and NON-NATIVE varieties, thus implying that human lin-guisticality is differentially operative in the two sets of varieties. In response, Singh demonstrates that what are regarded as breakdowns of communication across cultures are in fact attributable either to assumptions of cultural (= ethnic) superiority (producing what he calls DEAFNESS) or to differential language proficiency, and that the effects of the differential language proficiency are easily overcome if there is a measure of charity, humanity and rationality. He also challenges those who assume synchronic qualitative differences between NATIVE and NON-NATIVE varieties of English to produce evidence to justify their assumption.

Seen from one point of view, these lectures on sociolinguistics concentrate on denying significance to a series of prevalent lines of enquiry (perhaps, all the major ones) in the field, thus suggesting that they are in fact lectures AGAINST sociolinguistics. It is, however, important to remember that they are only against what is at present projected as sociolinguistics, and that they give, in the process of criticising current work, enough indication of a different, for me much more powerful and promising, concept of what sociolinguistic enquiry can be concerned with and what its rewards might be. Further, all of Singh's criticism of current lines of enquiry is strictly rational and logical, and any current work in any field of enquiry should become fitter for having had to face rational and logical criticism. After all, variation studies which take due account of (the possibility of) human linguisticality can add significantly to our understanding both of linguisticality and of the range and the limits of language variation; and cross-cultural communication studies which frankly face assumptions of cultural/ethnic superiority can usefully probe the relationship between language proficiency, cultural difference and genuine failure or repairability of communication. I therefore believe that these lectures have the potential to be a major milestone in the progress of sociolinguistics, either in its current forms but on healthier lines or, even more exciting, in newer forms in the future.

Bangalore
November 1, 1995

N.S. Prabhu

PREFACE

This book consists mostly of edited transcripts of the handful of lectures on sociolinguistics I gave at the National University of Singapore during the winter term of 1992-93. A few of them were also presented, later, at the Universität Graz. I am grateful to K.P. Mohanan and N.S. Prabhu of N.U.S., Singapore, and to Bernhard Hurch of Universität Graz for their invitations to share my reflections with students at their institutions. I am also grateful to the scores of bright, young Singaporeans and Austrians who allowed me to persuade them to consider the possibility of unlearning some of what they had learnt. This group included, I'm confident, some we will hear more about before the end of this century.

One of the lectures I gave could not be, unfortunately, recorded — technologies other than variationism and generativism also have their own limitations — and two of the lectures I was planning to give were pre-empted by more important things — sociolinguistics, after all, is only a small part of life, even for sociolinguists. Though I am aware of the fact that no imagined audience can replace a real one, I have tried to write the latter two (lectures 3 and 6) as if I was delivering them to my favorite Singapore audience. The former (lecture 9) has been subtituted by a lecture on the same topic that I delivered elsewhere in Singapore. At the suggestion of some friends, I have added, as lectures 10, 11 and 12, slightly modified versions of talks I gave elsewhere: 10 was first given at the 1990 annual meeting of the Canadian Association of Applied Mathematics, at the Association's invitation, 11 was first prepared for the 1995 Conference on Political Linguistics of the Belgian Linguistics Association held at Antwerp, and 12 at the University of Chicago. These later additions create some repetition and perhaps some stylistic inconsistency, but, my friends insist, not enough to warrant their exclusion.

The lectures that follow are based on various papers on

sociolinguistics that I have authored or co-authored and, although they make very liberal use of these papers, I have decided to preserve the oral flavour because it allows the reader to see clearly how linguisticality and sociality engage in the interplay that constitutes the sort of socio-linguistics current paradigms seem to discourage one from undertaking.

The pedagogicality of the oral style makes these lectures, in my view, eminently suitable for students, and they are my primary intended audience, just as they were in Singapore. I am confident, however, that practising sociolinguists will have enough to sink their teeth into, and the book will allow them to appropriately train the next generation.

As my own conception of sociolinguistics is summarized by Prof. N.S. Prabhu in his foreword to this volume — I am grateful to him for writing it — with an articulate elegance I cannot match, I shall not say anything about it here. I need, however, to share my response to why I am, as he puts it, "fiercely critical" of most of what passes for socio-linguistics. I am critical for the reasons he provides. I am fiercely so perhaps because I am surprised not so much at those who do what most of us call sociolinguistics but at us who call it that. I do, however, plead guilty to the charge of not having discovered a more polite way to evaluate things that mock man's linguisticality and ridicule his sociality. As far as exaggeration is concerned, and there is some in these lectures, I exaggerate only to reveal the hidden contours of what I examine. The only valid tribute to thought, as Foucault once said, is to use it and to make it groan and protest.

Whether my defense against Prof. Prabhu's entirely justified characterization of the tone of what little I have to say makes any sense or not is for the reader to decide. Precisely how justified I think Prof. Prabhu is is reflected in my decision to call this volume not, as I had originally intended to, LECTURES ON SOCIOLINGUISTICS, but *Lectures Against Sociolinguistics*.

Having borrowed his AGAINST, I must sign an IOU. I am happy to, but the only one I can sign honestly can say only that some day I hope to be able to put a volume together I'd be happy to call LECTURES ON SOCIOLINGUISTICS. Hopefully, one of the bright young people I lectured to during the winter of 1993 and the summer of 1995 will produce such a volume before I do, and get me off the hook.

I hope you have as much fun reading these lectures as I had delivering them.

Montréal
May 15, 1996

Rajendra Singh

INTRODUCTION

The aim of this volume is to critically examine the dominant ways of doing sociolinguistics, sometimes taken to be sociolinguistics itself, and to sketch out the outlines of the alternative ways such an examination persuades us to entertain seriously. The critical examination I undertake pushes the dominant ways of doing sociolinguistics to the point of crisis. Whereas these ways project a picture of sociolinguistics as a sub-discipline in which unexamined language surfaces are correlated with unexamined social appearances, I attempt, through their critiques, to construct a picture of sociolinguistics as a space in which the speaker claims her sovereign right to conceive of her language in critical/rational terms. Assuming that "linguistics" is about underlying processes that make languages "tick" and sociology is about NOT taking social appearances for granted, I argue that any sociolinguistics that does not meet these requirements of linguistics and sociology cannot be taken seriously. I also argue that most of contemporary sociolinguistics must be rejected and transcended because of its preoccupation with the regulative. A meaningful sociolinguistics must deal with the constitutive instead.

In the first three chapters, I show the limitations of the variationist enterprise in phonology, semantics, and sociology. I argue that too much is assumed rather than demonstrated to be variation, and that once higher principles of phonological (prosodic) and social organization are taken into account what the variationist enterprise presents as phonological and social "variables" can no longer be construed as such.

In the next three chapters (4-6), I look at the laboratory of language contact and attempt to show that neither the standard contemporary sociolinguistic view that there are no non-social constraints on the results of contact nor the standard formalist (or generative) view that contact is only a peripheral phenomenon can be sustained. I argue that a meaning-ful socio-linguistic account of contact cannot be constructed without taking into account the constraints imposed by our linguisticality, something as real as our sociality.

In the next two chapters (7-8), I attempt to show that by restricting itself to symptoms and by refusing to come to terms with power, contemporary interactional sociolinguistics merely reaffirms the facticity it claims to address. What it offers as "the cause" for communicational synchrony in inter-ethnic and inter-sex communication, I argue, is simply the linguistic evidence for the causes it refuses to even recognize.

In the lecture on so-called "new/non-native" varieties of English (chap. 9), I argue that the distinction native/non-native has no pertinence for these varieties, for they represent shared systems that by definition make their users native speakers. There is, in other words, reason to say that speakers of Texas English are not native-speakers of R.P. but no reason to say that speakers of Yorkshire, Texas, or Singapore English are not native speakers of English. In this lecture, I attempt to expose the equation: English = Standard British/American English, and the paradox that it is the so-called sociolinguist who takes away, ironically in the name of social responsibility, the pride conferred by the linguist's naive attribution of the designation "native-speaker".

In lectures 10 and 11, I take up (1) the lexicographical discourse of dictionary definitions, again something I consider to be an important part of sociolinguistics and (2) Chomsky's delineation of what he calls Orwell's problem, which I take to be a part of sociolinguistics. In the former, I attempt to show that what started out as an aid to the unskillful in the 17th century has long since become an aid to the skillful only. In the latter I argue that the Chomskian distinction Plato's Problem/Orwell's Problem may not be as clear-cut as Chomsky thinks it is.

In the last lecture, entitled "Statistics and the Structure of Language", I attempt to show why the favoured metalanguage of contemporary sociolinguistics, the language furnished by probability theory, cannot in principle account for human sociolinguisticality.

It is important to underline that most of these lectures are AGAINST only what is generally projected and taught as sociolinguistics. In focussing on that projection, I have, unfortunately, ended up ignoring other voices and ways that are available to anyone willing to listen and explore new paths. Some of theses have been put together in Singh (1996a). The challenges against that projection presented in the lectures that follow join those voices and ways, and contain the outlines of new ways of exploring the space that could legitimately be called socio-linguistics. Those oulines are quite transparently the focus of some of these lectures — the lecture on the dictionary as an introduction to sociolinguistics, for example, explores the familiar space of lexicography in a manner in which it is, I believe, normally not explored. This book is, in other words, intended for the next generation of sociolinguists, which, in the words of Fishman (1992), should not be allowed to rest content with linguistic complacency and sociological naïveté.

1. VARIATIONISM—I

> *Rather, the question should be "what are the principles that determine the observed factor structure."*
>
> K. Hakuta 1984: 230

I shall begin with the distinction between regulative and constitutive rules because most of what I have to say assumes a very clear understanding of that distinction. I summarize some of the properties of these two kinds of rules in (1) below:

(1) Regulative (R) and Constitutive (C) Rules (R)

	RR's	CR's
(a)	Certain things ought to be, may be, or are done	How are things done?
(b)	If P, then Q	What counts as P?
(c)	The activity is independent of RR's	The activity is logically dependent on CR's
(d)	Presuppose CR's	Do not presuppose RR's
(e)	Do not generate new behaviours	Generate new behaviours

The differences noted in (1) above can be elaborated as follows:

a) regulative rules tell you how certain things ought to be done or how certain things may be done or how certain things are actually done. As opposed to this, constitutive rules tell you how things are done. They don't tell you how certain things ought to be done, or how certain things may be done, but how things are actually done.

b) The second difference between these two classes of rules is that regulative rules always have the logical form IF P THEN Q, whereas constitutive rules tell you what counts as a P. They don't tell you that if P is present then Q must ensue. They tell you what a P is or what linguistic or social behaviour is actually to be counted as a P.

c) Another distinction between these two classes of rules is that as far as the regulative rules are concerned, an activity, which could be linguistic, social, cultural, socio-linguistic or socio-cultural, is completely independent of them. It is completely independent in a logical sense. There is no logical dependency between the activity in question and the set of regulative rules that could be used to describe a part of it.

As opposed to this, an activity is logically dependent on constitutive rules. You can't perform an activity which is logically independent of the constitutive rules that characterise that particular activity or set of activities from which that one is taken.

d) Another distinction between these two types of rules is that there is a logical asymmetry between these two because the regulative presupposes the constitutive. You can have regulative rules only under the condition that there is a set of constitutive rules that characterise that activity, but constitutive rules do not presuppose any regulative rules. It is perfectly possible to have a set of activities which must be characterized in terms of a set of constitutive rules but these activities don't have to have an associated set of regulative rules.

The last difference, which is crucial to most of what I'll try and look at in these lectures can be summarized somewhat as follows. Regulative rules do not generate, don't produce, do not account for, whichever expression you prefer, new behaviours; they merely describe, old observed behaviour which can be broken down in terms of variables, in terms of factors, in terms of contextual conditions of various sorts, but they do not, indeed cannot, generate new types of behaviour which have not been observed, which have not been recorded, which have not been subjected to any sort of factor analysis. As opposed to this, the basic, fundamental property of constitutive rules is that they generate, produce, automatically account for, or provide you with a blueprint for understanding new behaviours that have not been observed, that have not been recorded or analysed with any standard set of analytical tools. This distinction is very important for us.

If you look at the set of social-linguistic behaviour and you describe it with the set of the analytical tools that your theory provides you with, you can only describe that which has been observed. The defining property of constitutive rules, on the other hand, is, I repeat, that they account for things that cannot in principle be observed. This is a very important distinction, and you'll see some of its implications as we proceed to look at some particular constructs in sociolinguistics.

I'd like to begin with the construct called the VARIABLE RULE. It is a tool that has been in use for 30 years and is still used very productively in various analyses of human sociolinguistic behaviour. I'll begin with an examination of a particular data-base taken from English. Consider (2) below, which contains data collected by Wolfram (1974), who studied some American adults.

Text	**Context**
The food is wonderful	___ +V
The food smells wonderful	___ –V
We agreed on that	+stress
We cárried a box	–stress
That's the wrong side	–morph
I wonder why he sighed	+morph

(2) Some Data on Variation in American English

The first pair has *The food is wonderful* and *The food smells wonderful*. The second pair consists of *We agreed on that* and *We carried a box.* The third pair consists of *That's the wrong side* and *I wonder why he sighed.* You will notice that there is a contrast that characterizes these three pairs of sentences. The distinction between the members of the firsts pair can be characterized by saying that the obstruent /d/, the sound that may be left out in the actual pronunciation of these two sentences, appears in two different cotexts. Remember the distinction between co-text and context. By co-text, I mean the linguistic context that is available in the sentence. The word *food* in the first sentence of the first pair is followed by the word *is*, which begins with a vowel, and that is its co-text. That is what you see on the extreme right-hand side of (2). It says +V, which, in ordinary English prose, is understood as: "it is followed by a word which begins with a vowel." In the second sentence, the word after *food* begins with a word that begins with a consonant. That is formally stated on the extreme right hand side of (2) as __-V, which means it appears in a cotext in which the next word does not begin with a vowel.

In the second pair, the word that contains the sound /d/ is distinguished in the first and the second sentence by the feature or the property that is described on the right hand side of the table above. So that in this case, the sound appears in a syllable that carries the accent, the main stress of the word. In the second case, the sound that we are interested in, /d/, is not contained in a syllable with an accent. The members of the third pair are distinguished by the fact that in the first sentence, the sound /d/ does not have any grammatical functions, it is not a morpheme — it does not, in other words, indicate any special morphological properties of the word in which it appears. The word *side* is made up only of one morpheme. In the second sentence in the pair, the sound /d/ is found as a tense marker, i.e., it has independent morphological function. To summarize, in the first case the sound /d/ does not have morphemic status of its own; in the second case, it does have a morphemic status.

Now if one looks at pairs of sentences like these, one could construct what is called a product display for them. It is given in (3) below. It is taken from Fasold (1991), which is an attempt to relate the variable realizations of a particular sound. If you look at the product display in

(3), you'll find the facts of the matter to be concisely displayed. Remember that we are looking at the sound /d/ and what we want to find out is whether the sound /d/ is retained or deleted.

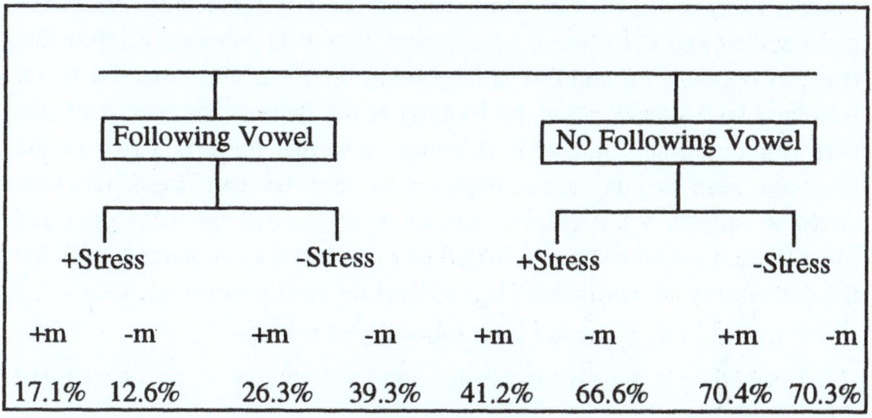

(3) Product Display

The major deciding factor seems to be whether the sound that we are looking at is followed by a vowel or not followed by a vowel. The second major criterion that allows us to make a distinction of sorts is whether the sound to be deleted is contained in a syllable that carries the main accent of the word or whether it is contained in a word or syllable that does not have an accent. The deletability or retainability of the sound seems also to depend on whether it constitutes a morpheme by itself or it is merely a sound with no morphological function or morphological status. Identical decisions can be made in the context where it is not followed by a vowel, and if you look at a rather large body of data in American English what you'll find is something of the sort that I have indicated in the last line. So that you find, for example, in 17.1% of cases when the sound actually constitutes a morpheme, iappears in a syllable that carries a stress mark and has the property that it is followed by a vowel, then it is gotten rid of, it is not pronounced, 17.1 percent of the time. Compare this with what happens when there is no following vowel. If the sound "d" constitutes a morpheme by itself, has some morphological status, is in a syllable that carries the accent, and appears in a cotext in which there a is vowel, then it is deleted, not pronounced 41.2

percent of the time. Now you can compare these figures across the product display in (3) above.

If, for example, the sound does not constitute a morpheme (does not mark a morphological function), appears in a syllable that carries the main accent and is followed by a vowel, then it is deleted 17.1% of the time, as opposed to, and this is important, 66.6% of the time if it is not followed by a vowel. Thus, by looking at the facts of the matter of this sort, one could say that what is going on is that there is a rule in the language, and in this case it happens to be American English, which could be called a VARIABLE RULE, a rule which will say that word-final /d/ is to be deleted, to be eliminated or to be left unpronounced, and that the deletability of word-final /d/ is subject to three main conditions:

1. followed by a vowel or not followed by a vowel;
2. whether it appears in an accented syllable or in an unaccented syllable;
3. whether it has an independent morphological status or not.

One could write a rule of the kind that appears as (4) below, where the rule simply says that word final /d/ is variably deleted — it is not always deleted, but variably deleted (i.e., depending on these three conditions). Now one can take these conditions and these percentages, translate them into probability figures, depending on how large a body of data you have, perform a multiple regression and then write a fairly sophisticated rule. I'll look at that degree of sophistication later if warranted but for now (4) is sufficient for what I want to do:

(4) $d \rightarrow \langle \emptyset \rangle / C_1, C_2, C_3$ (where C_1, C_2, C_3 represent the conditions enumerated above)

Now, consider the assumptions that are made in this analysis. There are essentially two: (1) that /d/ and /ø/ or /d/ and silence constitute the same entity. These are assumed to constitute the same unit or the same thing for social and linguistic purposes. So, the first basic assumption can be summarized as in (5):

(5)

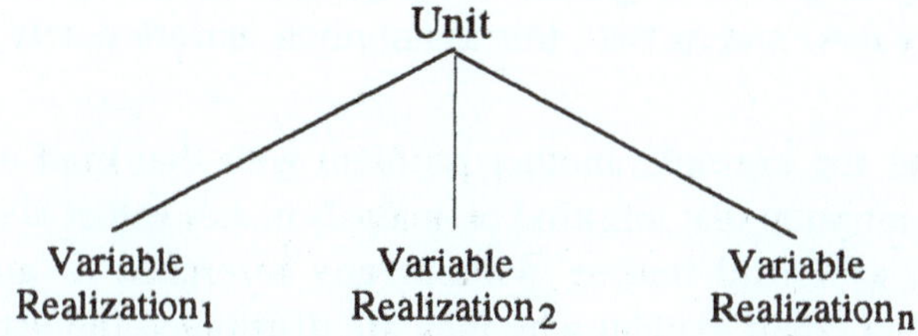

Alternates, in other words, are studied set-wise independently of their rôle in the system they are a part of. They are also studied without reference to any guiding principles.

So you look at two alternates, in this case /ø/ and /d/. And you assume they must have the same role in a system that they are part of. What is meant by the expression "they have the same role in the system" is that speakers of this particular language, speakers of this particular dialect, speakers of this particular variety construe, imagine, think, or live with the illusion, if you like, that silence is the same thing as /d/ in this particular context.

Now, consider somewhat more complicated cases. Consider the word *test*. Now this word by some speakers in some regionally localized languages is pronounced as /tɛ s/. Now some speakers say /tɛst/ and some speakers say /tɛs/. Our first inclination would be to say that these /t/ and ø are alternate realizations of the same sound: in one case the sound is realized as /t/, in the other case it is realized as zero, just as we saw in the case of /d/ and zero. Now notice there is an interesting twist to this logical assumption. Suppose that we find it empirically to be the case that a speaker who says /tɛs/, pronounces its plural as /tɛsəz/. And there are speakers like that, perhaps on the wrong side of the Atlantic, but they certainly exist. For these people, the singular, I repeat, is /tɛs/ and the plural is /tɛsəz/. Now, notice for these speakers it may not make any sense to say that the sound /t/ has been deleted from the word *test*, because for these speakers the /t/ is perhaps really never there. If it was, you would expect them to say /tɛ s/ in the singular and /tɛsts/ in the plural, but what they actually say is /tɛs/ in the singular and /tɛsəz/ in the plural. That means that variable-rule analysis has to rely very heavily on the assumption that when two alternates are being described as variants, they belong to the same grammatical system. In the cases in which speakers say /tes/ and /tɛsəz/, this assumption, unfortunately, cannot be maintained.

Consider for example another problem with that kind of analysis. Another assumption that this kind of analysis makes is that alternates can be studied, as I said before, without any reference to any guiding principles that could explain why they are distributed the way they are. Consider the fact that in most dialects of English the words *history*, *density* and *anarchy* can be pronounced in such a way that the second vowel, counting from the left, is not pronounced. You can say /hɪstri/, you can say /denstɪ/, but you can't say /anrkɪ/ easily. Now, one could say that these are the cases from which the vowel has been removed in a variable fashion. I could say that in a large corpus, one finds a rather large number of cases of the first kind, a moderate number of cases of the second kind and a very small number of cases of the third kind. What I could do, again hypothetically, is guess that the probability that the vowel will be deleted in *history* is 8, on a scale of 0 to 10. It has extremely high probability. In a word like *density* the probability is more like 5, again hypothetically. In a case like *anarchy*, the probability is very low, let's say, 1. I could further add that in casual, informal fast speech this is what is likely to happen, so when one speaks in an informal fashion one is likely to delete the vowel and when one is very careful and cautious in one's delivery then the vowel will not be deleted. But the interesting thing here is to ask the question why should that be the case. If I only give the probability and say that the deletion or the alternation of the vowel with zero is probabilistic, I am not asking the question why should that be the case.

Now consider the facts of the matter. For example, if in the first word I delete the vowel, what I have between the two vowels is /s/, /t/ and /r/. Notice the consonantal cluster or the group of consonants /str/ has the rather interesting property that /st/ can appear in the coda of an English word like *past* and that the consonantal group /tr/ can appear in the onset of an English word, so we can say *tray* meaning that the three consonants that appear between the two vowels can be analysed either as constituting a single consonantal coda and a double consonantal onset or a double consonantal coda and a single consonantal onset. Contrast this with the second word. It gives you /nst/ between vowels. Notice that /ns/ can terminate a word in English so we have a word like *prince* and the consonantal group /st/ can begin a word such as *storm.* Contrast both of these words with the third word. What we have there is /nrk/. That is a very interesting group of consonants. There is no word in English that ends with /nr/. It is impossible for an English word to end with the cluster /nr/, unless the /r/ is syllabic. It is equally impossible for an English word to begin with the consonantal group /rk/. There is something very peculiar in the three consonants that appear in the third word as opposed to the three consonants that appear in the first two words. Suppose one were to say whether something happens very frequently or not so frequently is really a function of whether what is left can be properly understood as part of the language system. If what is left when something has been deleted constitutes a proper part of the phonological system of the language, then you can do it. If what is left is of a nature that takes some liberty with the system of the language, then you better be careful.

Notice that if we make a distinction of that sort, we know that in words like *history* there is no problem — you can delete the vowel anytime you like; in words like *density*, be a little careful because what is left is somewhat marginal though legal; in the third case the language may even offer its apologies. The point here is: if you understand the principles that explain this behaviour — when the vowel is to be deleted — there is no need to talk about something called a variable rule. Or, to put the matter differently, what is sometimes described as a variable rule is simply a very superficial effect of some guiding principles of the system of the language in question. If one understands what those principles are, one would never have the need to talk about variable rules. Here the principle is quite simple. It is if the consonantal residue that you are left with after deleting the vowel is such that it can be parsed as possible onsets and codas in the language, then you are allowed to do it. If what you are left with is such that it cannot be parsed as a possible combination of onsets and codas in the language, then you don't have the license to perform that operation. Computing the probability of these things will turn out, I would like to suggest, not to be a fruitful exercise because the results can be predicted on the basis of general principles.

Now consider (6) below, a more general rule of this sort which has been proposed in the literature. It describes certain facts about the behaviour of word final consonants in general:

(6) [+ cons] → <Ø> / <[+ cons]> <Ø> __ <# #> <[- sy]>

The rule asserts that the variable rule of C-deletion will operate more often if

(a) another consonant precedes it

(b) it is not followed by a word beginning with a vowel

This rule has been taken from an eminent American sociolinguist, William Labov. He proposed it in 1971 (and repeats it in Labov 1987). He says that essentially there is a general rule in English: do not pronounce (delete) a word final consonant under the set of conditions given above. What is important to understand is what is behind the formalism. This rule, which allows you to alternate a word final consonant with zero, is subject to two conditions. One, that it will operate more often if another consonant precedes it and (condition 2) if it is not followed by a word beginning with a vowel. We should ask the questions we asked before: that is, why is it sensitive to a preceeding consonant and why it is sensitive to a following vowel?

These questions are merely rhetorical questions in the sense that we have already looked at the answers. So we know why it is sensitive to a following vowel, we know why it is sensitive to a preceeding consonant. Because of the kinds of consonantal groups that will result should we decide to do something with the word final consonant.

Now take a phrase like *dump Lisa.* Notice that it is possible to take the /p/ of the first word and transfer it with a sandhi operation or what the French or Romance tradition calls LIAISON; you can take the /p/ of the first word and add it on to the second word. You will have /dʌ mp liza/ which is in fact an allegro realization of *dump Lisa*. The point again being that there are general principles of organization, called *sandhi* or *liaison*, which tell you when you can perform this kind of operation with word final consonants and when you cannot. If those principles are clearly understood and can be clearly described as a systematic aspect of phrase phonology, it becomes a redundant exercise to say that these facts of the matter must be described with the help of variable rules. There is nothing in the behaviour of word final consonants either in English, or in French or in Spanish or Sanskrit which will allow you to say these things in an autonomous sort of way. Whatever happens in these languages is a logically necessary consequence of the rules of sandhi that operate in these languages, making such statements of variability redundant.

Now we could perform the same kind of exercise with so-called social variables. One could say that X is realized as Y in the presence of a certain set of social variables, represented below by $[V_1]$ $[V_2]$ ......$[V_n]$:

(7) $X\_ \langle Y\rangle / [V_1]\ [V_2]\ \ldots\ldots\ [V_n]$

One finds in socio-linguistic descriptions of the sort we have been considering, statements that say: delete this sound or don't, or alternate this sound with some other sound in formal speech but don't do it in careful cautious speech. One also finds statements of the kind that this or that is done by uneducated speakers but it is not done by educated elite speakers of the language. One describes these features as + or – educated, + or – elite, or + or – upper-class and so forth, as if they were independent, autonomous variables. The point is if there is a general understanding of why that should be the case, we'll not have to state such things or stipulate them as autonomous variables. If one could, for example, adopt a general principle, derivable from a social theory, which says that elites tend to formalize their discourses, then it wouldn't be necessary to use features like ±educated, ±upper-class as autonomous entities, because it would follow directly from general social theory.

But there is actually a more complex problem associated with the formulation of such socio-linguistic variability in terms of features. The general problem, as Kandall (1981) points out, has the following shape: if B_1 is a particular behaviour caused by some social variable V_1, then it must be the case that an unexpected or unchartered behaviour is caused by some unchartered variables $V_n \ldots V_{n+1}$. If this appears too abstract, let me go over it again. What is being said is: if we can describe socio-linguistic behaviour in terms of variables, things like education, age, sex class affiliation and so forth, we are committing ourselves to the view that if we find unexpected behaviour, it must be the result of the presence of some unexpected social variable(s).

Consider an encounter of the following sort. You go to a car salesman and you present yourself as somebody who needs a car. During the discussion, the car salesman finds out that your name is Raj Singh. In the American context it is quite possible to imagine the salesman saying "It is really nice talking to you Raj" which, as an Indian, I find somewhat vulgar. I don't like to be addressed by people by my first name unless I have known them for some time. I ask myself: what to do in a situation like this? My response would be to address the salesman by his last name. Now a standard socio-linguistic analysis of this will say that this must be the result of an unexpected set of variables. Or, suppose, for example, that you have a daughter who is 18 or 19. If she dresses up extremely well on some evening you might say "Miss Singh, you are looking absolutely glorious tonight." It is not that you generally address your daughter with her last name but because you as a father are threatened by the fact that she is likely to go out of your life, and you want to capture the combination of affection and irony by addressing your daughter by her last name, saying in effect, that you know that she is about to go and you also want her to know that you ARE her father. Now this combination of things, which is part of the constitutiveness of your being a speaker of the language cannot be described in principle by isolating a finite number of variables because they do not tell you what you are likely to do in an unexpected context. The real problem is not in the anecdotes that I have narrated to you but in the problem of infinite regression. That's why most socio-linguistic studies typically must end with statements like "we need to look at more data", "we need to examine a larger population", or "we have to isolate more variables."

They all end up saying "some evidence is still lacking" or something like "although we have examined a rather large number of variables the total number of variables is extremely high." They invariably end their discussion with an analysis of the socio-linguistic facts of the matter by an apology of this sort. If one was charitable, one could say that this is an understandable apology and the investigators are merely indicating to the reader that a lot of work is still to be done. If one were uncharitable, one could take the position that these all translate as "please give us more money so we can carry on our research on more people." I'll leave it to you to decide which of the two interpretive comments you prefer. The charitable one acknowledges that this researcher has worked very hard, this is what he has analysed but a lot of work remains to be done. The uncharitable one is that the investigator is really saying "I want to look at 3000 more people, three hundred more societies, so please give more money." The basic conclusion I would like you to think about is that the defining parameters of the constitutive rules of socio-linguistic behaviour cannot be understood merely by isolating a finite, though extremely large, number of variables, because they create the problem of infinite regress.

The general conclusion must be that our constitutiveness as social-linguistic beings cannot be captured, cannot be formalized in terms of a finite number of variables, irrespective of how large the number of variables we have been able to isolate is. You can take 300 variables or 3000 variables, but that will not amount to defining our constitutiveness. Our constitutiveness must be predicated on what we can do in unexpected cases, in unexpected circumstances for which we have not been prepared. That is what makes us social-linguistic beings. Variables can capture part of what we "normally" do, but that can't be of any interest, except perhaps to Ann Landers or Emily Post.

2. VARIATIONISM—II

> *It is thus that new semantic, expressive, paralinguistic and kinesic features of behavior involving speech have been isolated, providing us with a new bagful of indicators to do something correlational with.*
>
> E. Goffman 1964: 133

Let us begin with the basic problem that the method that we looked at in the first lecture tries to solve. The basic problem of variation is that it exists and that it must be described. No one has ever denied that variation exists. We must find ways and means by which we can describe what can be called language variation. More important than the fact that variation must be described is the fact that it must first be established. In order to describe variation one has to show that there is variation. One must ask certain questions about what constitutes an example of variation and what does not. In relatively abstract terms you can visualize it in the way represented in figure (1) below:

(1) An Abstract Representation of Variability

a) b) c)

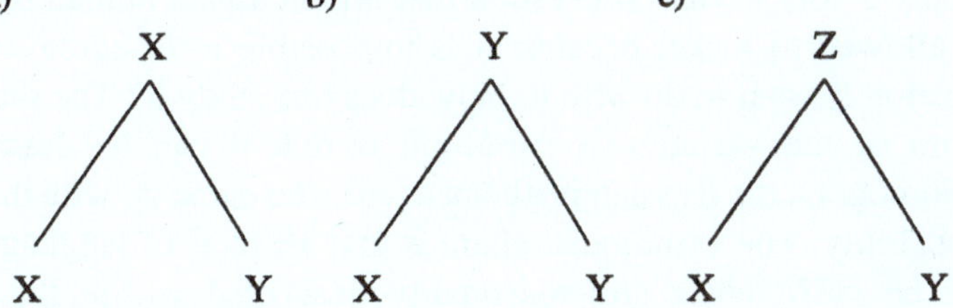

Figure 1 says if you find an X which stands for something and a Y which stands for the same thing, then they are variables which are related because they both come from X. If one wants to say that X and Y are two variants or are related by variation, this can logically be the case only under three circumstances: (i) when X and Y can be seen as realizations of X itself, (ii) when X and Y can be seen as realizations of Y itself, or when one can postulate some abstract entity and say that it has two shapes — sometimes it has the shape of X and sometimes it has the shape Y. So, in order to talk about variability, it is important to realize that we must make a very fundamental assumption, and that is the assumption of sameness. It is impossible to talk about variation unless we assume that at some level of analysis, at some level of perception, at some level of reality, these two or three things that we want to say are variants of each other must be related in some such way that they can be construed to be the same thing. Having made that clear, the second step we must take is that we must establish that that sameness actually exists. If we cannot show that it exists, then we cannot talk about variation. If we cannot establish it, we are not talking about variation. We are actually talking about two different things not related via variation. This will become clear as I take up actual, concrete examples.

Now the study of the problem that I have just sketched out before you within the paradigm that is normally referred to as variationism — the paradigm or the method responsible for the construct variable rules — can be summarized in the following manner. It makes or accepts the very trivial observation that variation exists. I repeat, it is impossible to quarrel with that observation. That observation merits the comment that Pauli used to make to young people who would come up to him and say obvious, common-sensical things. It was *Das ist nicht einmal falsch* or, in English, *that is not even false*. The observation that variation exists is simply a very trivial observation that no intelligent human being should be allowed to make, because it is impossible to disagree with it. The question is what to do with it. How does one study it? The second major claim of the variationist paradigm is that it can be described *à la* Kolomograv, the Russian mathematician who came up with the theory of probability. The variationist claim is that all facts of language variation can be sufficiently and reasonably described within the theory of probability. The application of the theory of probability is based on the fundamental assumption that any object one wants to study can be decomposed into a set of finite variables. If you cannot decompose your object of study into finite variables, then probability will not work. We have already seen that the kinds of things we are interested in as socio-linguists cannot be broken down into a set of finite variables.

The next observation about the variationist paradigm I want to make is that even if it could be described in that way, i.e. even if we grant that facts of a socio-linguistic nature can be described as variables, then we have to ask the question exactly what is the status of that description? There are two possible responses to this. First, there is the strong response, which says speakers actually internalise the raw probabilities of things that happen in their language. That response says, essentially, that there is some ontological status to be attributed to frequencies and probabilities that one finds in a language and that speakers actually internalize those probabilities. Nobody subscribes to that view. The weak response, on the other hand, admits that we do not memorize, we do not internalize, the raw probabilities but asserts that we do memorize, we do internalize, we have access to, the implicational relations that one can obtain by looking at probabilities. The claim is that in essence what we do know is that certain things happen very often, certain things happen quite often, and certain things happen not all that often. There is an implication or generalization that one can extract from these raw probabilities. What the speakers have direct access to is this kind of implication, not the raw probabilities.

What WE have tried to do, as you saw in the last lecture, is to argue that in fact the content of the weak response can be derived, can be predicted, without recourse to probability. I remind you of the examples like *history*, *density*, *anarchy*. The results that we saw can be computed without counting things, without taking probabilities into account, on the basis of other principles.

Let me refresh your memory by giving a somewhat more detailed analysis. Let's consider these cases again. We have the three words *history*, *density*, *anarchy*. In (2) below, I have broken their post-deletion variants down according to their syllabic composition:

(2)

	hi $ stri
histri	hist $ ri
	his $ tri)
	*de $ nsti
densti	den $ sti
	dens $ ti
	*æ $ nrki
ænrki	*æn $ rki
	*ænr $ ki (with non-syllabic /r/)

What you see in (2) above is something like this. If you remove the vowel, what you have between two vowels in the first case is the consonantal cluster /str/; in the second case, you have /nst/; in the third case, you have /nrk/. This is after the vowel has been removed or has been deleted. Now if you look at these consonantal groups, you'll find some very interesting things, some of which I described in the last lecture. We can look at them in detail now.

Notice what is left in the first case can be decomposed either as /st/ followed by a syllable boundary, followed by an /r/. We say -/str/- can be decomposed as /-st$r-/ because there are words like *lost* in English that end with /st/. Notice it can also be decomposed as /s$tr-/ as is shown by fact that English has words like /trick/ which begin with the consonantal group /tr/. In the second case, you can decompose the consonantal cluster either as /ns/ + syllable boundary + /t/, or as /n/ + syllable boundary + /st/. We can do the first decomposition because English has words like *prince* and we can do the second decomposition because English has words like *star*. In the third case, the sequence of consonants cannot be decomposed in that manner. There is no word in English which ends with /nr/ (where the /r/ is non-syllabic) and there is no word in English that begins with /rk/. So, we know that the contingencies of English phonology would not easily allow you to syncopate in the third case, though they will in the first case quite easily.

Interestingly, there are some speakers of English who do not make a distinction between the word *prince* and the plural of the word *print*. For these speakers, the two words are identical. So *prince* is pronounced in exactly the same manner as the plural of *print*. If you take the name of

German airline *Lufthansa*, the second syllable in the name of the airline is for these speakers of English identical with the third person of the verb *to hunt.*

They are incapable of saying /ns/ at the end of a word. They must say /nts/. Now these, the intermediate cases, demonstrate, independently of any theory of probability, that cases of this type must be placed between examples like *history* and examples like *anarchy*. We can, in other words, construct an implication scale just by looking at these facts, without worrying about who deletes what on Wednesday morning and who deletes what on Thursday afternoon after a hot cup of tea. We do not have to look at those factors because the relevant facts follow directly from the phonological properties of the language.

Now what I'd like to do is turn our attention to the second presupposition. That is the assumption that what is being compared is the same entity. I will first take a lexical example. If one were to take a word like *exhausted* and a word like *wiped out*, one could say these are variants of each other. The word *exhausted* has some meanings M_i, M_j and M_k. *Wipe out* also has a rather large number of meanings associated with it, let's say, X, Y, Z. In this particular case, what is important is the fact that one specific meaning of *exhausted*, Mj, in this case is the same as the meaning Y associated with the word *wiped out*. That meaning, let's say, is *tired*. This implies that the range of meanings that can be associated with *exhausted* overlaps with the range of meanings that can be associated with *wiped out*. Because of this overlap, one might want to say that these two words are merely variants of some other abstract meaning. Unfortunately, *exhausted* does not mean, cannot mean *demolish*; *wiped out* can and does. If we make the assumption that these two words, *exhausted* and *wiped out*, are merely variant realizations of some other abstract entity and that they can be studied or perhaps should be studied as two variants of the same meaning, the gap just noted will show that that assumption is, as Lavandera (1978) points out, not justified. Only *wiped out* can mean *demolish*. The first word, *exhausted*, cannot mean *demolish*, and that almost destroys the hypothesis that these two words can be seen as variants of the same meaning or the same concept. Their ranges of meaning are very different, indeed.

Let me take an example from phonology to show the same thing. The data comes from an article by K.P. Mohanan (1992). He argues that there are some speakers of Singapore English that pronounce the word written as *help* and the word written as *sulk* in the manner indicated below:

(3) [heup]
[sauk]

The associated words *helping* and *sulky* are, however, pronounced by some with an [l], i.e., with no vocalization of the lateral consonant, and by some others without the [l], which is turned into a vowel in these words.

(4)		
	[helpɪŋ]	[heupɪŋ]
	[salki]	[sauki]
	V(ariety) 1	**V(ariety) 2**

Let's look a bit more carefully at the speakers who vocalize the /l/ in both sets of words. Both the words *help* and *helping* in their speech will be pronounced without the [l]. A variationist could quite easily say these are actually variants of each other and the difference between these two varieties or dialects V1 and V2 can be explained or described by saying that V2 has a rule which says that [l] becomes /u/ in specific types of codas. Let's call this rule J. In V1, the claim will be made, rule J does not exist. This could well be the variationist's description of the facts of the matter.

The interesting fact is, Mohanan argues, and absolutely correctly, that there is reason to believe that there is an [l] in V1 but none to believe that there is one in V2. Speaker of V1 can therefore be said to vocalize the [l] because sometimes it shows up, as in the case of *helping*, and sometime it does not, as in [heup]. As far as the speakers of V2 are concerned, it never shows up. The [l] is just not there. If the [l] is not there, either in [sauk] or in [sauki], it does not make any sense to say that it has been turned into a vowel. The right position to take is, it seems, that there isn't any [l] there to begin with. There is no reason to say that for the speakers of V2 there is an [l] either in [sauk] or in [sauki]. The correct analysis would be to say that the underlying form or the form that the speakers of V2 must have in their mental representation is a form without the [l].

The reason this example is important to understand is that it underlines the importance of sameness. One could describe it as an example of variation, but only under the assumption that at some level of analysis they constitute the same entity. But we have seen in this case that they do not constitute the same entity. If they do not constitute the same entity, they cannot possibly be analysed as examples of variation.

Let me take an example from syntax. It is based on Harris (1984) and is a bit complicated. If you bear with me, you will, however, see what the assumption of sameness allows you to do. In Irish English, it is possible and legal to say things like *She has nearly her course finished*. It is impeccable, well formed legal English. If one wanted, one could say that it is nothing to write home about; it is a very simple variant of Standard British English (SBE). The minor difference is that the participle form appears after the direct object in Irish English but it appears in another place in SBE. If this was Standard British English, one would say *She has nearly finished her course* rather than *She has nearly her course finished*. So, on the face of it, it looks like a very simple variant of what one would say in Standard British English. On the basic of this example, one could hypothesise that the only difference between Standard British English and Irish English is a low level movement rule which simply says. "Take the participle from its place in SBE and move it to the end." That's how you get an Irish English sentence. One could analyse these two sentences as variants of each other by claiming that the only difference between the two is the movement of the participle to the end of the sentence.

Now consider some very interesting facts about Irish and British Engish. In Standard British English one says

(5) Peggy has swallowed an orange.

In Irish English one says

(6) She has nearly her course finished.

The sentences above can be, unfortunately, compared only if the intended interpretation is resultative in nature. So, *Peggy has swallowed an orange* and *She has nearly her course finished* are comparable only under the semantic interpretation I am, following Harris, calling resultative. That's the kind of semantics that this sentence expresses in Irish English.

Now consider how what some grammarians have called HOT NEWS is expressed in these two dialects. In Standard British English one says

(7) A young man has just got shot

For HOT NEWS in Irish English, one does not use that structure. Instead, one says

(8) A young man's only after getting shot

This means that although the perfect in standard British English looks like the perfect in Irish English, by the time you get to the hot news the similarity has disappeared and a difference has come in.

Consider the semantics of *extended now*. In Standard British English one says

(9) I have known them for 17 years.

In Irish English, on the other hand, one says

(10) I know his family all me life.

You do not use the structure instantiated by *I have known*; you use the simple present and say *I know*, instead. Again, the correspondence that seemed so important at the beginning between *Peggy has swallowed an orange* and *She has nearly her course finished* breaks down.

If you compare the semantic interpretive rules that are associated with the perfect in Standard British English and Irish English you will be forced to say that the perfect of Standard British English is not really comparable to the perfect of Irish English. Any attempt to say that Irish English Perfect is merely a variant of Standard British English perfect is in fact a mistake. It is a serious mistake because it is associated with an entirely different range of semantic interpretations than the range that comes with the perfect in Standard British English.

The main point of this demonstration is that in all three types of cases that we have looked at, drawn from the lexicon, phonology and syntax, the assumption of sameness did not turn out to be true. It was merely declared to be true in an *ex cathedra* fashion. You cannot merely look at a form and say that it must be a variant of another form you know from somewhere because it is from the same language. One must demonstrate that what is being analysed as a variant is in fact a variant. If it turns out that these things are related in such a way that they cannot be synchronically derived from some common source, they are not variants at all.

Going back to the schematic presentation of this, if you look at these two dialects of English, you cannot say that there is an X, such that the perfect in Standard British English and the perfect in Irish English must come from it. It looks very much like the Y of Standard British English comes from X and the Y of Irish English comes from Y. They don't share the same semantic or interpretative rules. They cannot, therefore, be analysed as variants of each other.

We have seen that in the lexicon, we have seen that in phonology, and we have seen that in syntax. It is much too easy to make the assumption of sameness and much too difficult to demonstrate that that must be the case. The point I'd like to emphasise is that before describing variation one must empirically show that variation actually exists in phonology, in lexicon, in syntax, or in any other domain of grammar. Yes, variation must be described — nobody will ever quarrel with that. But the description must be a description of something that can be shown to exist.

Principles like the sonority hierarchy and *sandhi* potential render quite a bit of the variability we have been looking at redundant. Principles like the one enshrined in the proposition that the dominant shall formalize their discourses renders it even more redundant. And some of it disappears because it cannot even be shown to be there, except under incomprehensible assumptions of sameness.

When one is talking about linguistic or socio-linguistic variability, a description of that socio-linguistic variability should contain that and only that which cannot be deduced from general propositions of the type we have looked at. If a socio-linguistic description contains that which is predictable, that which is deduceable from general propositions, then it is being extremely redundant and it is hard to see what purpose it might serve other than the purposes that we talked about last time. The final conclusion must be that any description of socio-linguistic variability must describe that, and only that, which cannot be predicted from general propositions either about language or about society. That which can be predicted, that which can be deduced, does not have to figure in the description.

Let me go back to the phonology example and explain a bit more precisely what I mean by *sandhi*-potential or sonority-hierarchy. That's why I wanted to keep them till the end. If you go back to the examples of *history*, *density* and *anarchy*, you find in the first case the coda is /st/ and the onset is /tr/ (/ns/, /st/ in the second case). Why am I saying all this is all predictable? You could say this is really black magic and Singh is simply asserting that this is predictable but it really isn't. So you want to see why this is predictable; in order to see that, consider the coda /st/ or the onset /tr/. There is a more general, universal principle according to which if there is a language L_j such that it allows two consonants word-initially, then it must allow /pr/, /tr/ and /kr/. Actually I don't know of any human language which allows two consonants at the beginning of a syllable, without allowing /pr/ and /tr/. Notice this is a fact independent of anything, at least independent of the sort of variability that we have been talking about. You might find languages in the world that do not allow two consonants syllable-initially. Punjabi, for example, is a language which does not allow syllable-initial consonantal clusters. You might find a language that does not allow any clusters initially. Walpiri is supposed to be a language of that sort.

But if a language allows two consonants in the initial position then those two consonants must necessarily include /pr/, /tr/ and /kr/. Consider an onset of the kind /rk/. To the best of my knowledge, there are very few languages in world that allow this. The incidence of that kind of onset is extremely rare in human languages, if not impossible. Perhaps even in the case of Kabardian and Czech one could argue that these are not really allowed.

The point is that /rk/ as a cluster in the onset position of a syllable is very, very rare, if not impossible. Why should that be the case? You could say that instead of pulling one rabbit out of the hat Singh has actually pulled out two. Consider the fact that in any human language and this has been known for a very long time, syllables have an interesting property. It is that segments or sounds in syllables are generally arranged in such a way that in the initial position, one goes from low sonority (or if that term appears to be technical, just think of it as musicality, or lack of noise), but in the final position, i.e., after the vowel,one starts reducing the sonority. This is a fairly general principle of the structure of syllables in human languages. The sonority hierarchy is merely a formalized statement of that.

Given these principles, we can predict, independently, I repeat, of any variability study, what kinds of implications must hold in terms of what can be pronounced and what can be deleted or what must be pronounced and what can be left out. Identical considerations, I shall try to show in the next lecture, apply in the context of social variables. If we have propositions that capture the nature and structure of human societies in intelligent ways, then what one says about social variables can also be deduced from general propositions of this kind.

What do we conclude from the picture I have presented here? In order to do socio-linguistics that may have some explanatory potential, what we need to do is to look for propositions about the forms of human language and to look for propositions about the nature and structure of our societies; deduce what we expect to find; and carefully, consciously, deliberately and, if necessary, painfully look for counter examples that will help us to revise these principles rather than merely go around with a camera and a tape-recorder and only record the situations as they obtain in various places. There is, unfortunately, no point in saying that Cambodians have two legs, Singaporeans have two legs, the British have two legs, and Americans have two legs. It is sufficient to say that homo sapiens has two legs. One should be busy looking for people that might have three.

3. VARIATIONISM—III:
The autonomy of social variables

> *Collective representation, emotion, and tendencies are caused not by certain states of consciousness of individuals but by the conditions in which the social group in its totality is placed.*
>
> E. Durkheim 1938: 106

Many contemporary sociolinguists have repeatedly emphasized the difficulties encountered in describing "the facts of the matter" in multi-layered, multilingual societies such as India and Africa (cf. Gumperz 1982a and b and Shapiro and Schiffman 1981, for example). The position they advocate *vis-à-vis* the complex facts of the Indian sub-continent, for example, is that they require an appeal not to theories of grammar produced in and for largely monolingual societies but to theories that take into account social conditioning factors and deal with code-repertoires and language variability *à la* variationism (cf. Gumperz 1976, 1982a and b; Kachru 1978; Pandharipande 1981; and Shapiro and Schiffman 1981, amongst others).

In this lecture, I shall attempt to show that the descriptive models used by these sociolinguists to ascertain the facts of the matter leave out some very fundamental questions about language and society (cf. Singh and Lele 1985, 1987, and Singh and Ford 1988). They are unable to even raise those questions essentially because they reduce both language and society to an un-ordered, unstructured set of independent variables and assume that the relations and orders amongst them will emerge after a large number of correlational studies are replicated over time and space. Guided by a very deeply-rooted empiricist bias, they assume that the descriptive categories they employ are non-derived primitives and that the facts of the matter ascertained by using these primitives call for no further comment or explanation.

I can clarify the point with two examples. Consider the variable rule of word-final consonant deletion, formulated as (1) below by Labov (1971:272) and discussed in the previous lecture:

(1) [+cons] → < ∅ > / <[+cons]> <ø>___<##> <[-syllabic]>

In the previous lecture, which was based on Singh (1987), Kiparsky (1988) and Singh and Ford (1988), evidence is provided to show that the variability of the linguistic features (indicated by < > in Labov's formulations) derives from certain universal principles of prosodic organization and need not be stated or stipulated anywhere.

Shapiro and Schiffman (1981:54) fault contemporary grammatical theory for not building into the structural descriptions of linguistic rules "social conditioning factors" and prefer the Labovian variable formulations in which variables such as age, education, +high (prestige) and +formal can be given their proper and rightful place. At several places in their comprehensively programmatic description of the Indian subcontinent, the variables +high and +formal co-occur, but that co-occurrence is of no interest in their model, just as the co-occurrence of word-boundary and the feature syllabic has no particular significance in Labov's formulation above. The explanation for the latter is offered by the prosodic principle that the reduction of the "weight" of the word, measured in terms of moras, is understandably, as we saw in the previous lecture, more difficult if what is to the right is likely to create a complex onset. The explanation for the former is available in a theory of society that predicts that the dominant will formalize their discourse habits and conventions.

The conclusion these examples force is that the variability model provides, at best, a heuristic for isolating "variables" that need to be referred to theories of language, of society, and of language-in-society in order to "understand" the complexity involved. "The facts of the matter", in other words, are not what they are without reason, the implicit assumption of the model seen as the only one capable of handling "the Indian situation."

In this lecture, I shall attempt to find orders and relations that exist in "the plethora" of linguistic code-distribution in India and seek an explanation for what current research in sociolinguistics, particularly within the variationist paradigm, would like us to believe are irreducible primitives. I shall argue that most of the "bewildering array" of phonological variables involved is grounded in some very general principles of prosody and rhythm. In this lecture, I would like to show that the social variables follow from a theory of society.

We cannot, in other words, afford to stop at what they consider to be independent variables. We also take the view that the relations and orders amongst these variables must be understood within the context of Indian society and that what needs to be undertaken is not, as Shapiro and Schiffman (1981:176) put it, detailed empirical investigations of "the kinds of phenomena now being done in the West" but a serious attempt to find reasons these variables pattern the way they do on the Indian subcontinent. I shall illustrate this with one rather detailed example.

One of the arguments advanced by the contemporary sociolinguist, particularly of the American variety, is that his view of language and language-variability is particularly, even uniquely, suited for describing complex Indian and African bilingual and multilingual situations, situations involving language-contact. I shall choose an Indian example. It has been inspired by such a perspective, which has been popular since Emeneau's (1956) classic paper that declared India to be a "linguistic area", fertile for claims regarding convergence, an idea that has resisted clear empirical verification in the European context. Our sociolinguist believes that the Indian evidence from contact-situations provides evidence FOR the correctness of his view and the incorrectness of views of language-structure, such as generative grammar, that refuse to recognize variability of the sort he studies as an inherent feature of language-design. He also believes that the incorporation of inherent variability of the sort that is, according to him, dramatically exemplified on the Indian subcontinent into the metatheory of language is crucial and critical in order to come to terms with language-change. I shall take Pandharipande's (1981, 1986) studies of Marathi from a sociolinguistic perspective as my example.

Even the title of Pandharipande's empirically rich paper of 1986 is revealing: "Language Contact and Language Variation: Nagpuri Marathi". It clearly indicates that it should be taken as a plea for the correctness of the contemporary sociolinguist's view of language. The first few lines of the paper set the stage even more clearly and forcefully :

> "In recent years, it has been argued variously (Bailey and Shuy 1973, Bickerton 1971, DeCamp 1971, Labov 1969 [sic], etc.) that the metatheory of language should incorporate variation into the core of language study. Empirical studies of Haugen 1953, Gumperz 1971, and others question the traditionally accepted monolithic concept of language. Diachronic as well as synchronic aspects of variation are discussed (Bell 1976, Hock and Pandharipande 1978, Kachru 1976, 1978, and Weinreich 1953). With this upsurge of studies on language variation, languages spoken by bilinguals have come to be looked upon in a very different light. Mutual 'interference' of the languages spoken by bilinguals is now regarded as a natural outcome of linguistic convergence (Fishman 1972). Bilingualism, among other sociological factors such as sex, class etc., thus plays an important role in bringing about variation in language. The dichotomy between monolinguals' 'pure' vs bilinguals' 'impure'/'deviant' speech is questioned." (219)

She advances a few arguments in favour of the claims indicated above and one generalized argument against the opposite view that rejects the enshrinement in linguistic theory of "factors" she considers important. We shall look at these in turn.

Her central claims are: (i) that the features that uniquely characterize Nagpuri Marathi are shared with and taken from Hindi (219), (ii) the sort of analysis she is able to provide of NM is made possible by the framework suggested in Labov (1970), Gumperz (1971), and Kachru (1976), (1978), and (iii) the NM facts of the matter present, in both synchronic and diachronic dimensions, insurmountable problems for other sorts of linguistic theories, the generative one in particular. First, here are the synchronic facts of the matter.

As is traditional, she begins with what are clearly lexical matters. Her argument is that NM has a sub-lexicon that it shares with Hindi and that is absent from Pune Marathi (PM). Some of her examples are given in (2) below.

(2)		a	b	c	d
		PM	NM	Hindi	Gloss
NOUNS:	1.	dār	darwāzā	darwāzā	'door'
	2.	ghar	makān	makān	'house'
	3.	divā	battī	battī	'lamp'
	4.	viḍā	pān	pān	'betel leaf'
ADJECTIVES:	5.	prāmānik	imāndār	imāndār	'honest'
	6.	vedā	pāgal	pāgal	'crazy'
	7.	rikāmā	khālī	khālī	'empty'
	8.	kaṭhin	muškil	muškil	'difficult'
VERBS:	9.	bhī-ṇe	ḍarne	ḍarna	'to fear'
	10.	varṣa-ṇe	baras-ṇe	baras-na	'to rain'
	11.	visar-ṇe	bhul-ṇe	bhūlna	'to forget'
	12.	āvar-ṇe	same-ṭṇe	sameṭ-nā	'to collect'
ADVERBS:	13.	ajibāt	bilkul	bilkul	'at all'
	14.	haḷu haḷu	āste-āste	āste-āste	'slowly'

There are several dimensions to the selection-bias of the lexical data she provides. It is clear that what has been done is that PM is represented by its high, formal, educated variety, and both NM and Hindi by their low-middle, informal, colloquial varieties. In (3) below, we provide some examples of lexical alternatives in Hindi and PM that underline her selection-bias:

(3) a. Hindi i) ghar 'house'

ii) dwār 'door'

iii) varsa 'year'

b. PM i) pān 'betel leaf'

ii) darwāzā 'door'

iii) khāli 'empty'

The trick employed, one is tempted to say, is to list only [+Sanskrit] items for PM and only [–Sanskrit] items for NM and Hindi. Actually one could argue that her list contains no examples from Hindi at all: they are all from what is generally referred to as Hindustani. Her observation, to which she gives the status of an argument, that the items in her list (cf. 2 above) are not exotic, specific-domain words but words "related to everyday life" (221) doesn't really help matters because we are not told whose daily life is at issue; the additional data in (3) indicate quite clearly that there are speakers whose daily-life is described by them somewhat differently than she would have us believe. We do not want to claim that NM has not borrowed a single lexical item from Hindi but merely that lexical borrowing cannot be established for multi-lexical grammars by crossing variety-style-register boundaries and that when one considers the same sort of speakers in PM and NM; "even" lexical borrowing diminishes in its import. We say "even" because lexical borrowing is known to be rampant. The real question, it seems to us, is not the extent of lexical borrowing from Hindi into NM but the paucity of it. That paucity is probably related to the fact that both Marathi and Hindi have what could be plausibly described as two different lexica, Hindi to the extent of giving rise to what is now, for obvious socio-political reasons, perceived and recognized as another language, Urdu (cf. Singh 1985a, Rai 1986, amongst others).

Her discussion of what she calls conjunct verbs is initiated by the same selectional bias. She cites the triplet *viśrāntī gheṇe* (PM), *ārām kar-ṇe* (NM) and *ārām-kar-na* (H) 'to take rest', for example, to claim that NM has conjunct verbs absent in PM and that these are modelled after Hindi. As far as "Hindi" is concerned *viśrām* is the corresponding form to PM *viśrānti* (at comparable levels of variety, style, and register); and as far as PM is concerned it is doubtful if *ārām* is ungrammatical in every register.

She also provides some examples of calquing (both at the lexical and "morphemic" level), but these present no serious challenge to any view that is willing to admit the existence of items that historically must be seen as having been borrowed, and, as far as we know, no theory of language has ever denied the possibility of lexical borrowing. As a matter of fact, lexical borrowing is so profusely attested that it seems almost pointless, at least from a general, theoretical point of view, to provide yet another list. The compound and conjunct verb cases would be of some interest if these were not merely lexical matters. That they are is acknowledged even by Pandharipande (222 and 223).

Her discussion of matters she considers non-lexical is equally fraught with undetected dangers. It is, for example, not clear why the choice of the verb *rāh-ṇe* as an auxiliary to mark the progressive tense instead of *as-ne* is a syntactic matter. Where similar choices are permitted within the same grammar, as in French, it is clearly a lexical selection: some verbs take *avoir* 'to have' and some *être* 'to be'. Both Quebec French and inter-standard Parisian-French quite often show that this lexical-selection boundary is crossed with relative ease. In the latter case, the monolingual child's environment contains no other language; in the former case, it contains the environment provided by English which provides no model for this "mixing of categories". Although Pandharipande shows that *rāh-ṇe* is not used as a progressive auxiliary in PM, she does not show that it can't be used as an auxiliary of any sort. But even if her demonstration that the use of *rāh-ṇe* as a progressive auxiliary in NM is modelled after Hindi is valid, the latter cannot be considered as anything other than lexical. Besides, the ontogenetically motivated use, or extension, of *rāh-ṇe* in the so-called progressive construction cannot be ruled out. It is interesting to note that the suffixation of the verbal stem (by *–t* in PM) is not dispensed with in NM (cf. PM *mhaṇat* vs *mhaṇūn* for example). The Marathi grammatical seal appears not only here but also in the case of adverbs allegedly borrowed from "Hindi", for what Pandharipande calls the "instrumental suffix" in these cases is *-ṇe* and not the Hindi *-se* (cf. NM *muškili-ne* and PM *kaṣṭane* vs 'Hindi' *muškil-se*).

Another allegedly syntactic matter she discusses has to do with negative polarity suppletion. In PM, *pāhije* and *nako* constitute a polarity suppletion pair: *pāhije* cannot appear in sentences containing the negation marker *nāhī* she says. She neglects to mention that *nako* cannot appear in such sentences either (cf. 4 below):

(4) *malā cahā nako nahi

I would prefer to say that *nako* is constrained to occur in sentences that are syntactically non-negative. If her characterization that it is *pāhije* that is so constrained is correct, it becomes difficult to explain why (4) above is ungrammatical. The claim that it is *pāhije* that is constrained is comparable to the claim that every verb in Hindi that can be used in the imperative is constrained not to co-occur with the negative *nahin* (the negative marker required in the imperative is *mət* in Hindi), a patently absurd claim. *Pāhije* has no constraints, as NM in fact shows; it is merely lexically supplanted by *nako* in PM, a local lexical matter in the extreme, perhaps comparable to the fact that *soda* in some dialects of English is *pop* in others, etc. Notice that NM provides crucial evidence for choosing between a constrained *pāhije* and a constrained *nako*, and not for a strange, grammatically inexpressible variability that must be enshrined in some pan-dialectal grammar that is real for native speakers of neither PM nor NM. The alleged peculiarity of NM trivially follows from the fact that it doesn't have the word *nako*. This makes a mountain out of a molehill!

Simple suppletion is also responsible for the contrast in (5):

(5) a. PM āmhi udyā mumbailā zāṇārnāhi
b. NM āmhi udyā mumbailā zāṇārnāhi
āmhi udyā mumbaila nāhi zāu
c. PM *āmhi udyā mumbaila nāhi zāu
'We will not go to Bombay tomorrow.'

As she provides no data on word-order constraints in NM, her claim that (5c) above is modelled, as far as the placement of the negative particle *nahi* is concerned, after "Hindi" is difficult to assess. The standard PM insistence on the suppletion *zau* by *zanar* is, however, clearly a lexical matter.

It is interesting to note that what Pandharipande presents as semantic evidence for convergence is exclusively a matter of lexical semantics. Her evidence is given in (6) below:

(6) PM		Hindi	
a. *bhaṭak-ṇe*	a) 'to roam around' b) *'to get lost'	*bhaṭak-ṇā*	a) 'to get lost' b) *'to roam around'
b. *mil-ṇe*	a) 'to get' b) *'to meet'	*mil-nā*	a) 'to get' b) 'to meet'
c. *pakad-ṇe*	a) 'to catch' b) *'to hold'	*pakaṛ-nā*	a) 'to catch' b) 'to hold

NM

d. *bhaṭak-ṇe*	a) 'to roam around' (PM) b) 'to get lost' (Hindi)
e. *mil-ṇe*	a) 'to get' (PM and Hindi) b) 'to meet' (Hindi)
f. *pakad-ṇe*	a) 'to catch' (PM and Hindi) b) 'to hold' (Hindi)

Her conclusion is that for these verbs the semantic range is largest for NM and smallest for PM, with "Hindi" falling somewhere between NM and PM. Although her somewhat arbitrarily imposed restrictions on the meaning potentials for these verbs in "Hindi" can be challenged rather easily — consider, for example, Hindi *vah dilli me bhatak raha tha* 'the was wandering around in Delhi' — our main point is that changes at the lexical semantic level are entailed by the possibility of lexical borrowing anyway, also perhaps because lexical semantics, as

Jackendoff (1983) shows, is, after all, not "semantics" in any linguistically interesting sense,for what is apparently responsible for it is our general conceptual apparatus. Be that as it may, it is enough to point out that what we have here is a simple case of lexical borrowing (formal and "semantic", if you like).

Pandharipande takes her findings as evidence for the following claims: (i) "the traditionally accepted theory of transformational grammar fails to account for such a linguistic situation", (ii) "variation in Marathi supports the claim that sociological factors such as bilingualism play an important role in language change" (220), (iii) the analysis provided is based on an "independently motivated theory of linguistic convergence", a theory according to which "languages in contact become more and more like each other" (229), (iv) the situation at hand supports the view, held, according to her, by Labov and Kachru, amongst others, that an adequate theory of language change should be made dynamic enough to accomodate sociological factors (230) and (v) contact has furnished NM with more than one way to perform the same grammatical function.

Before we take up these claims, we need to point out that although she is aware of the fact that investigations such as hers raise and must answer the question whether borrowed and native items and structures are extralinguistically in free variation — available to all speakers in all styles at all occasions — she does not (230). We have already suggested that they are not and her specific claims rest on her selection bias (towards the H in PM and towards the L in NM and "Hindi"). We shall, however, not belabour the point, and proceed to examine her conclusions despite these problematic distortions.

She believes that the generative view of language is not up to the task because (i) a generative account can have recourse only to loss, addition, and simplification of rules but what is involved in NM is, according to her, grammar complexification (229) and (ii) generative grammar is in principle incapable of explaining why the relevant changes have occurred in NM at all. Inasmuch as what is involved is mere lexical borrowing, we don't see the point of our first claim. What is at stake, in other words, is lexical enrichment of NM and not grammar complexification. The fact that certain locally definable structure types seem to have been enriched by what is seen as another means for performing the function they do poses no problem for multiple concurrentiality of means as the rule in human language, at least as far as morphology and syntax are concerned. We do not know of any language that has only one way of, for example, forming nouns from verbs or adjectives, or of asking questions, borrowing or no borrowing, irrespective of its history, in other words. Even if English hadn't borrowed from French, it would have at least two ways to nominalize adjectives (cf. *wide*, *width* and *good*, *goodness*) and German has half a dozen ways of pluralizing nouns, most of them very native indeed.

The objection that generative grammar fails to acknowledge that the relevant changes in NM are due to Hindi-Marathi bilingualism and to explain why they occurred at all (229) is curious, to say the least. We don't understand how *any* synchronic description of NM can "acknowledge" these peculiarities of NM as having been brought about in this way. Pandharipande's own paper enriches our understanding of the history of NM, but it is not a partial synchronic grammar of NM. As far as the diachronic dimension is concerned — why these changes occurred at all — the account provided by Pandharipande doesn't "explain" anything either. It merely notes the fact that NM lexicon was somewhat sporadically enriched by Hindi. An "explanation" will, minimally, have to deal with why it wasn't enriched in other corners and crannies. It is difficult to see the sense in which the observation that the lexicon of contemporary English is made up largely of non-Anglo-Saxon words can be construed as an explanation (of anything). Obviously, languages cannot enrich their lexica by borrowing from languages with which their speakers have had no contact. Equally obviously, languages WILL borrow from other languages they are in contact with. The interesting question there is: what is the direction of lexical enrichment and why? Consider, for example, the fact that it was ENGLISH that borrowed words from French a few hundred years ago but it is QUEBEC FRENCH that borrows FROM English today.

Those who today possess all the H registers of English are the social heirs of those who were bilinguals (English/French) yesterday. The tables have been turned for Quebec French for reasons those who talk about incorporating a social "factor" must seek to at least elucidate if not "explain" it. In the case at hand, what is needed is not a pseudo-incorporation of the sociological variable of bilingualism, but a comparison between Nagpur Hindi and NM on the dimension of lexical enrichment and an attempt to seek reasons for imbalances we are bound to find.

Other aspects of the Marathi case are examined in a preliminary way in Singh and Lele (1985). We argue that the functionally-oriented description of nativization variability provided in Pandharipande (1981) goes wrong on two counts: (i) in referring perfectly simple questions of linguistic form to speaker-attitudes and (ii) in not considering stalling and facilitating of borrowing as sociopolitical activities about which questions such as "Whose Marathi?", "Who was in contact with whom?", "When?", and "Why?" must be asked, in assuming, in other words, that attitudes arise and exist in the autonomous domain of a historically defined culture.

Pandharipande (1981) claims that (i) loans are never completely nativized in Marathi, (ii) there is a hierarchy of nativization of loans from Sanskrit, Persian and English, and (iii) this hierarchy is explainable on the basis of the attitude of the Marathi speakers towards Sanskrit, Persian, and English.

The first claim is obviously false, for Marathi is full of completely nativized Sanskrit words. As far as the other two major claims are concerned, I would like to suggest that what is construed as the hierarchy of nativization is in fact a function of two rather simple facts: (i) that borrowed words must first be assigned to a morphological category and a declensional class within that category, and (ii) that borrowed words that do not have a *svarabhakti* vowel, the crux of the hierarchy of nativization, because of prosodic reasons have it for entirely morphological reasons. It is easy to illustrate that the alternative is fraught with dangers because it does not exhaust the possibilities provided for by the autonomy theory. It claims, for example, that English *bus* and *doctor*, when borrowed into Marathi, do not take the locative suffix *-t,* as it would create unacceptable codas. The solution suggested is the postposition *madhe*. Native-speakers of Marathi could, potentially, render the unacceptable /bəst/ and /dɔktərt/ acceptable by inserting an epenthetic vowel in the unacceptable coda, but, it is claimed, they don't do this because their attitudes are such that they want not to treat English words in ways they treat their native lexical stock. The existence of words like *postat*, an entirely predictable consequence of prosodic principles, casts very serious doubts on the power attributed to those attitudes.

Looking at this power from the other side — the social side, that is — it has failed, despite the many efforts on the part of some native speakers to replace these words with Marathi words. We would like to suggest that the native speaker of Marathi uses the prosodic principle of *svarabhakti* — as does the native speaker of Hindustani, Turkish, Iranian, and Walpiri (cf. Singh 1985a) — to incorporate words from whatever source, just as he uses it to syllabify unsyllabifiable morpheme concatenations that arise in his native sub-lexicon — that is if, and only if, morphology forces his hand. Once they have become his, it is his rationality that frustrates attempts by elites to take them away from him for THEIR reasons.

To take an example from morphology, it is argued that the Old Indic prefix *a*-, though it may be added to native Marathi nouns and adjectives, produces ungrammatical results when added to English loans such as *doctor* and *smart*. The claim is comparable to the claim that the Romance suffix *-ity* in English is held at bay by English speakers at will. The fact is that *a*- is no longer a rule-introduced prefix in any Indic language, including Marathi. It doesn't appear as a prefix either with English loans or with Persian loans such as *khuš* and *majedār* for that reason. The fact that Persian affixes such as *-dār*, *ger*- and *bin*- can appear freely with both native lexical items and words of Persian origin shows that these affixes are gradually taking over the entire lexicon and not that Marathi speakers are attitudinally keeping the English and Marathi sub-lexicons apart (cf. Singh and Kully 1982).

Her other observation that words borrowed from Sanskrit resist most of the phonological changes which Sanskrit words have undergone in the history of their transition is merely an awkward paraphrase of the *tatasama/tadbhava* distinction long-established in Indic and Romance philology, and doesn't show what she believes it does. Affixes like *ati*-, *anu*-, *a*- ('up to') and *prati*- that appear in these words are not Sanskrit affixes borrowed into Marathi but unanalyzed, frozen chunks of these words that have no process-status in Marathi. And neither does the *izafe/svarabhakti* vowel of borrowed *tel quel* Sanskrit compounds.

The morphological and phonological nativization of non-native words in Marathi, we believe, shows that although contact can bring about changes in redundancy-oriented static aspects of grammar, it cannot easily touch its process-oriented aspects; speaker-attitudes can at best hold borrowing at bay, and both stalling and facilitating are socio-political activities about which another set of questions, such as whose Marathi? who was in contact with whom? and why? must be asked.

The point I want to make is not that the analysis in question is wrong, but that all such analyses are caught on the horns of a dilemma. Their functionalist orientation, unfortunately, guides them away from considering and exhausting grammatical possibilities as well as from asking questions the answers to which may lead to a theory of society. Some of the greatest linguists of our time have been caught in the functionalist trap. Martinet, for example, still believes that the /s/~/z/~/əz/ alternation in English is morphological despite the fact that the devoicing of /z/ is also seen in the possessive and the third person singular, and the *svarabhakti* vowel appears everywhere it is needed (cf. Martinet 1984). Lesser linguists don't even have his consistency and his modesty not to attempt to reduce society to attitudinal grids and multivariate matrices.

Not unlike other hybrid domains, sociolinguistics runs into several difficulties because it tries to operate with an *ad hoc* mixture of categories and concepts. If we are to go beyond this impasse, it is imperative that the problems of the sort we have looked at are examined afresh with theoretical and empirical vigour.

The sociolinguistic literature is full of such problems. Take, for example, the puzzle raised by Nadkarni (1975). As the apparently motiveless (structurally, that is) reborrowing or reactivation of the temporarily suspended inherited pattern of relativization is discussed in Singh (1986), I shall concentrate here only on the SOCIAL puzzle it raises. Nadkarni rests his "motivelessness" argument on linguistic grounds (i.e., that Konkani has a fully developed Indo-Aryan system of forming relative clauses) — a claim that Singh (1986) disputes on grammatical grounds. He then goes on to discuss some sociological factors, such as code-switching which is generally associated with prestige. He concludes that Kannada has no prestige in the region and hence the borrowings are based on the FUNCTIONAL DOMINANCE of Kannada. In spite of the sophistication of such sociolinguistic analyses, some basic sociological questions remain unexamined. Take, for example, the following:

1. What is the relationship between "functional dominance" and "social prestige"?
2. Why and when does "functional dominance" necessitate modifications to the prestige variable?
3. How do different classes among the Kannadigas perceive the claims of Saraswat Brahmins about higher social status?
4. What is the MATERIAL basis of functional dominance and the IDEOLOGICAL basis for prestige claims?
5. What are the historical reasons for the presence of Konkani-speaking Brahmins in a Kannada region?
6. What changes have occurred and are occurring at both the ideological and material levels in the relationship between Konkani Brahmins and the different classes of Kannadigas?
7. What is the general nature of class-caste differentiation in this society?
8. What impact do the changing socio-economic relations (of production, surplus appropriation and consumption, as well as of power) have or are likely to have on linguistic interactions, and what linguistic and social limits can we foresee for these changes?

It is not difficult to see that such questions necessarily arise out of a concern for an integrated theory of language and society. There exists a significant body of literature that analyses the evolution and structural bases of brahmanic status claims and juxtaposes them to the "non-standard", countercultural evidence arising out of folk literature and folk interpretations of social history and reality (for example see Omvedt 1985, Gupta 1980). In the particular case of Konkani as well as with Marathi and its regional variants, answers to these and other similar questions will provide us with a basis for a more integrated theoretical argument about the relationship between language and society in South Asia.

Another example is furnished by the sociolinguist's analysis of aspects of Hindi. In the case of Hindi the variability in the use of Perso-Arabic phonological units such as /f/ or /z/, and in the use of "pleonastic" relative-clauses, seen as arguments by Shapiro and Schiffman (1981: 54) for the variability model, in fact raises questions of the following sort:

(i) What, if any, is the difference between standard North American variable realizations of *Bach* [ba:k] and [ba:x] and Hindustani variable realizations of [bəzar] and [bəǰar]?

(ii) Is it enough to say that the variables that "regulate" the distribution of the invitational-tag are "socio-economic background" and "formality of the context" (Shapiro and Schiffman 1981: 54).

(iii) Why does the description of the notorious schwa-deletion problem in Hindi invoke features such as [±Native], [± Perso-Arabic] and [±Formal] at the same time?

4. LANGUAGE-CONTACT—I: *Contact and Phonology*

> *Grammar is not to be taken as the prescriptions of a legislator, at last giving the chaos of utterances their constitution and laws ... it is a discipline which states the rules to which any language must conform for it to be able to exist.*
>
> M. Foucault 1969: xiii

What I'd like to do in this lecture is to begin looking at some micro aspects of language contact. We will begin with the exploration of the micro aspects of language contact with phonology. In order to begin a discussion of language contact within the domain of phonology, one needs to understand two or three basic things. Once that background is clear, then the discussion of specific problems on phonology can proceed. So what I will try to do is to indicate to you how language contact or contact between two phonological systems or, two languages that may be involved in contact (very often there might be more than two, but I am taking two to be the prototypical case) can and should be studied. Now if two phonological systems or two languages are in contact with each other, one can look at that contact either from the purely synchronic point of view, the point of view of speaker at that time and at that place, or one can look at that contact in terms of the diachronic dimension, which deals with what the system of the language used to be like before it came in contact with another language. And if you look at the contact situations from these two points of view, you get a somewhat different picture. So that if you look at it from the synchronic point of view, the only distinction that you can make is between what you might call borrowed items and non-borrowed items. If you are looking at the language system or phonological system from the point of view of speakers at that given time, you can only make a binary distinction. You can make a distinction between words that have been borrowed and words that have not been borrowed.

If you look at words that are coming from another language, call it L2, then you can have essentially four kinds of words. In English, for example, if you pronounce the famous German musician Bach's name with a /x/ rather than with a /k/, then you have borrowed the name with German phonology. If you take a word like, let us say, Sanskrit /pənč/and pronounce it pretty much as it is pronounced in Sanskrit, then you could call it an incorporated item. No change is made to it in English. It just happens to be a Sanskrit word but presents no problem for speakers of English. It is taken *tel quel*, "as is". Now let's take the Indic word *saree*. In Indic languages it is pronounced with a retroflex, but some minor modification is made to the /r/ when it is taken into English. The word is, in other words, adapted according to the laws of pronunciation of English, and that makes it an adapted word.

Synchronically, the division would appear basically to be a binary one: words that have been borrowed *tel quel* i.e., that contain either sounds or patterns that are not typical, or perhaps not even permitted in the language, and other words that have beeen adapted or domesticated by the language which they have come into. Notice that incorporated or adapted words are, synchronically, not borrowed words. There is no reason to call them borrowed words because they are really part of the language system and they are part of the phonological system. Synchronically there is no reason to suppose that they COME from anywhere: they obey the laws, conditions and rules of the language in which they have been incorporated or adapted.

To call the words belonging to these categories borrowed follows from two kinds of considerations. It can follow from the diachronic consideration. The reason that one says that the Sanskrit word *punch* is a borrowed word in English is a historical reason. Such a statement simply says that there is a stage of English language in which the word *punch* is not there and later it is followed by a stage in which the word *punch* is there. It is a diachronic statement to say that word *punch* has been borrowed into English. Irrespective of where it is borrowed from, in the synchronic sense it is not really a borrowed word at all because there is nothing about the word that tells you that it is not an English word.

Identical considerations would indicate, for example, that after the form *saree* has been adapted according to the rules and conditions of English, to say that it is a borrowed word is to make an historical statement. Synchronically there is no indication in the word that would tell you that it has been borrowed. There is nothing in the phonology or the phonetics of the word that there is something alien or something strange in it.

It makes sense to talk about these things as borrowing under the diachronic interpretation and also under the functional interpretation. If one takes a functional perspective, one wants to say that in order to meet certain kinds of functional needs a language goes out and borrows these words from other languages. All of these — borrowed, incorporated and adapted items — constitute a single category, a single supra category, which for functional reasons can be called the CATEGORY OF BORROWED WORDS. It is important to keep this distinction in mind because the borrowed items actually raise questions of how bilingualism is transmitted in a community and how one learns another language either *in toto* or in parts. It also creates the possibility of what is called RELEXIFICATION, a term used to describe what happens in some contact situations when the borrowed items overwhelm completely the native words in the language to such an extent that the native words actually begin to fall into disuse and the foreign ones begin to take over.

The non-borrowed words raise questions regarding what is the language pattern i.e., what the phonological system of the language is, and how these words have been adapted. This might seem a bit abstract or a bit general. Let us, therefore, relate this to some specific facts. In (1) below, you have some words that Hindi has taken from English:

(1)	station	[Istešən]	slipper	[sIlIpər]
	spelling	[Ispəliŋ]	sleeping-bag	[sIlIpIŋ]
	school	[Iskul]	frock	[fIrək]
	sphere	[Isfiər]	fruit	[fIrut]
	speech	[Ispič]	flirt	[fIlərt]
	spoon	[Ispun]	pfizer	[pəfayzər]
	screw	[Iskru]	cloth	[kIləθ]
	stool	[Istul]	please	[pIlIz]

The English word *station* in this language is adapted as /Istešən/,whereas a word like *slipper* as adapted as /sIlIpər/. If you go down the list, on the right hand side what you see are the adapted forms of these words in this language.

If you look at all these words, you'll find something very interesting. The English consonantal cluster /st/, in the left hand colum is broken up with a vowel that appears before the /st/, whereas in the right hand column the consonantal cluster /sl/ is broken up by inserting a vowel between the two consonants /s/ and /l/. In Western Hindi, you don't say /sItešen/, you don't put the vowel between /s/ and /t/. And as far as *slipper* is concerned, you don't say /IslIpər/. If you go down the list, you'll see that there are two patterns. There are two strategies which have been used in this language in order to adapt English clusters, so that in some cases the vowel is inserted before the cluster and in some others it is inserted into the cluster. One does not, for example, say /Ipli:z/ one says /pIliz/.

The question is why should that be the case. Why is this language doing these strange things? Sometimes it inserts a vowel before the first consonant and sometimes after the first consonant. The facts of this language are not really isolated, and in order to see that the patterns exhibited here are quite general, take the English word *school* and consider what happens to it in Warlpiri., Hindi and Penjabi. In Warlpiri, a language spoken in Australia, it shows up as /kul/, in Western Hindi it shows up as /Iskul/ and in Punjabi and Eastern Hindi it shows up as /səkul/. The vowel is inserted between the two consonants in the case of Eastern Hindi and Punjabi, before the consonantal cluster in Western Hindi, and in Walpiri the /s/ is just dropped or deleted.

Or, consider the English word *snake*, which in Walpiri is pronounced as /sənek/, so the cluster /sn/ at the beginning of the word is broken up by inserting a vowel between /s/ and /n/. Contrast this with /kul/ where the vowel is not inserted between the /s/ and the /k/, or before the /s/. The /s/ is just gotten rid of. The contrast exhibited is that in Walpiri you have two patterns: (i) drop the first consonant (if your language does not allow it and if you are faced with an English word that you have to adapt to your language). It also uses the strategy which says don't drop the consonant but insert a vowel between two consonants (recall that *snake* becomes /sənek/).

As opposed to this, notice what happens in Western Hindi, which also has two ways of adapting English consonantal clusters. One is to insert the vowel before the first consonant as in *school* and the other is to insert the vowel between the two consonants as in /sənek/. As opposed to that, what happens in Eastern Hindi and Punjabi is that both use only one way to incorporate or adapt these words into their phonological systems, so that in case of both *school* and *snake* (you get /səkul/ and /sənek/), the vowel is introduced BETWEEN the two consonants.

Here one can begin to ask why this should be the case. For example why does not Walpiri do what is done by Western Hindi? Why doesn't Walpiri say /əskul/ or /ɪskul/ rather than drop the /s/? The reason that Walpiri does not do that is because if Walpiri were to do it, it would violate a general law of Walpiri which says words do not begin with a vowel. That's why Walpiri cannot take the option taken by Western Hindi. Because if it were to say /əskul/ it would be violating a general phonological law of Walpiri which prohibits words beginning with vowels. That's why it is forced to drop the /s/, while in Western Eastern Hindi and Punjabi that option is available because there are words that begin with vowels. What is interesting about these patterns is that they allow one to ask why in the case of Walpiri and Western Hindi there are two methods? Why doesn't Walpiri do the same thing with *snake* that it does with *school*? Or why does Western Hindi do one thing with *school* and another with *snake*?

Part of the answer, surprisingly, may lie in English, in a very indirect sort of way. Consider the following facts of English. For related reasons you have to emphasise a word like *Christ* in something like *For Christ's sake, leave me alone* as /kərayst/. Notice that what one does in English, in very emphatic speech, is to introduce the vowel between /k/ and the /r/. On the other hand, if you want to do something to an expression like *Please leave me alone*, you can introduce a vowel between /p/ and /l/: *Pelease get out of here*. Notice you can't do that with the word *stupid* in the expression *What a stupid mistake*. You can't put a vowel between the /s/ and the /t/. The only way to emphasise that in English is either to syllabify the initial /s/, or to geminate it, or to lengthen it. You can say *What a ssstupid mistake!* You can make the /s/ longer, but you can't put a vowel between /s/ and /t/. If you go back to Walpiri or Western Hindi, they are doing the same thing. Notice, for example, if you say /pɪliz/ in Western Hindi you are inserting a vowel between the /p/ and the /l/ just as in *Pelease leave me alone*. At the same time if you contrast that with something like *station*, what is being done there is that the vowel is being introduced actually before the /s/. The reason that it is being introduced before the /s/ is that Western Hindi does not allow syllabic and geminate /s/ — the laws of the phonology of this language do not allow you to lengthen it. What is going on in Western Hindi in the case of words such as *station*, *spelling*, *speech*, *spoon*, *stool* and *screw* is comparable to what is achieved by lengthening the /s/ in English.

The point is that there is a general distinction between things like /st/, /sp/, /sk/, on the one hand and /fr/, /sf/, /kl/, /sl/ on the other. These words can be divided into two categories, one where the vowel is introduced between two consonants and the other where the vowel is introduced before the first consonant. The question to ask is what is common to the facts of English, Walpiri, Western Hindi etc. In the situation of contact, what is it that decides where the vowel is going to be introduced if the consonantal cluster of English is not allowed? To find an answer to that, we will go back to what we mentioned when we were talking about variable rules, something that you should be extremely familiar with, i.e. the famous "Sonority Hierarchy." I display it below:

(2) p, t, k ... ... l, m, n, r, i, e, o ..... a

The Sonority Hierarchy

The sounds of languages can be divided into roughly five or six categories. The ones on the extreme left /t/, /k/, are the least sonorous and the ones on the right are the most sonorous, with other sounds falling somewhere in between. Sounds like /f/, /v/, /s/, /θ/, are more sonorous than /p/ /t/ /k/ but less sonorous than /n/ /m/ /l/ /r/. What do we do with the sonority hierarchy? What we can do with it is to incorporate it into a system of syllabification which is given below:

(3)

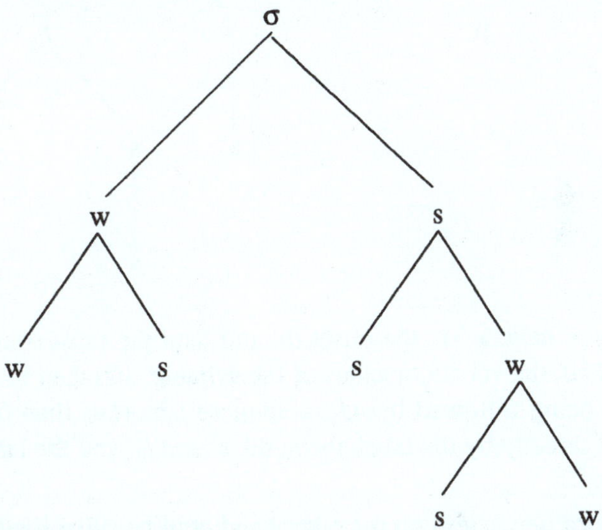

It says, essentially, that a syllable has two parts, the first part is expanded in a way that a segment to the right is more sonorous than the segment to the left. **W** stands for weak and **S** for strong. **W**(weak) means less sonorous and **S**(strong) means more sonorous. So in the onset of a syllable the segments should be arranged in such a way that the sonority is continually on a rise, till it hits the peak, which is the nucleus (a vowel). After that, in the coda of the syllable, the sonority begins to decline. You can perhaps look at it this way: it says that if you have a sequence like *past* and a sequence like *priest*, in general (i.e. in any human language) they will be syllabified respecting (2). A sequence of sounds like *past* is going to be syllabified as indicated in the tree below:

(4)

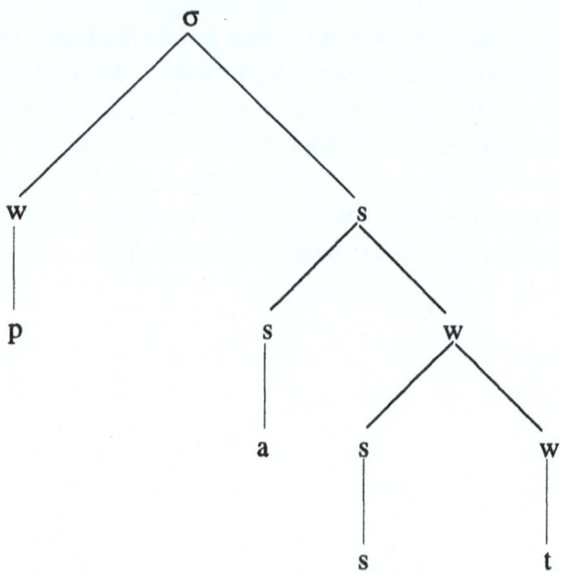

So you have a **W**, the onset /p/ and then the most sonorous sound, which is /a/, the vocalic nucleus of the syllable, and then in the coda you have /s/ being followed by /t/. /s/ is more sonorous than /t/ and that is captured directly by the label above the sound /s/ and the label above the sound /t/.

A word like *priest*, on the other hand, will be syllabified as indicated in the tree below. /p/ will have **W** above it and /r/ **S** above it (more sonorous). The sonority in the coda declines and in the onset it increases, as it is supposed to be in unmarked cases. English keeps this unmarked syllabification because it does not violate any of its phonotactic constraints. Another language may make certain adjustments to (5), if its phonotactics are violated, but we need not concern ourselves with that possibility here. In other words, there is nothing to write home about in (5) as the English syllabification of *priest*. The syllabification in (5) is simple, expected, and quite natural.

(5)

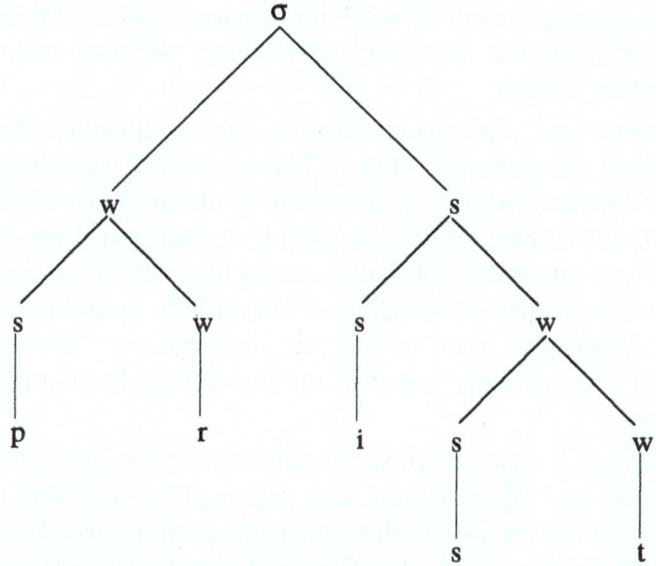

The assumption here is that in all human languages this is the kind of syllabification pattern that is available and exploited, except that there are two types of special provisions that need to be made for particular languages. The first exception or the first provision that one has to make is for things allowed by the universal syllabic template but accidentally not attested in a particular language. In English, for example, there are no words that begin with /mr/ or with /nr/, although these will be allowed by the Universal Syllabic Template, for /r/ is more sonorons than /m/ and it is also more sonorous than /n/. It is an accidental fact of English that it does not have words that there is no reason to disallow.

What follows from the fact of these accidental gaps is easy to see. Notice, for example, if you have a cluster /vl/, which, one could argue, does not exist in English, as in the name *Vladimir* (from Russian), a speaker of English language will have no problems with that: whether /vl/ exists or not in English is almost irrelevant. A Type A provision, therefore, is simply an indication of what the systematic gaps in a language are. That's why they generally constitute very good targets for the other language, so that if the other language has something which is allowed by the universal syllabic template but is not allowed by the receiving language, then the receiving language will incorporate these words very quickly and very efficiently, without making any modifications to them.

A second type of provision, which is somewhat more problematic, is also needed. Sometimes, what is highly marked according to the universal syllabic template is accidently or exceptionally perhaps permitted in the language that one is looking at. Notice that onset clusters like /sp/, /sk/, /st/, which violate the sonority hierarchy because /p/, /k/, /t/ are less sonorous than /s/, are allowed in most Indo-European languages. Most of them have word initials /sp/, /sk/ and /st/. This has to be stipulated and explicitly stated in the phonological systems of these languages.

What does it mean in terms of implications for contact phonology? And why are we looking at these facts in term of contact? This allows us to come to some conclusions about the kinds of strategies that languages use in order to adapt words from another language. Notice for example, that the first conclusion that we can safely drawfrom the facts of the sort that we have looked at, is that you insert an epenthetic vowel before the strong segment, before the more sonorous segment. Another conclusion we can draw from these facts is: if in any language, more than one strategy is used, as we saw in the case of Walpiri or Western Hindi, then sonority considerations have to play a role. If this conclusion is warranted, it should be impossible to find a language which uses more than one strategy to adapt words from English or from any other language without making these strategies sensitive to considerations of sonority. A language may, of course, have one simple way of adapting the prosodic structure of the words it wants to borrow (like Punjabi and Japanese). Punjabi and Japanese don't really care. If you take an English word and plug it into Japanese or into Punjabi, the solution is very simple and straightforward: put a vowel between the two consonants (and that's all you have to do).

But if you have a language that uses more than one way of handling clusters, like Walpiri or Western Hindi, then they have to be sensitive to sonority considerations. Now if you go back to Walpiri, you will notice that Walpiri deletes the /s/ in the case of word like *school* but does not delete it in a word like *snake*. The reason it does not is that the /s/ in *snake* is less sonorous than /n/. As far as /sk/ is concerned, it is an exception to the sonority hierarchy. So Walpiri's rule is to delete the segment if it violates the sonority hierarchy, and to insert a vowel between the two if it respects the sonority hierarchy. In that way, it is very different from Japanese and Western Hindi.

The third conclusion that we can draw from these facts is that the languages that do not allow any complex W's (complex onsets or complex codas) are likely to use only epenthesis. The reason that Eastern Hindi and Japanese use only the strategy of epenthesis is because onset and coda structure in Japanese and Eastern Hindi is very simple. In Japanese, only nasals and geminates are allowed as moraic segments. And Eastern Hindi does not even allow those. Hence, if the structure of the syllable is very simple, almost trivial, then and only then, are you likely to find a language in which only the strategy of epenthesis (put a vowel between two consonants) will be used.

The last empirical conclusion that one can draw from what we have looked at is: if you find a language which uses the device or the strategy of putting a vowel before the consonants, as in Western Hindi, where *school* becomes /ɪskul/ (the strategy of prothesis), then it must necessarily also use epenthesis. The empirical hypothesis that we can deduce from that is very simple: if you find a language that uses prothesis, then it must necessarily also use epenthesis, or, to put the matter differently, you can find a language that uses only epenthesis or a language that uses both epenthesis and prothesis, like Western Hindi, but you will never find a language that uses only prothesis. Test cases for our central claim will be languages like Turkish and Spanish, which sometimes borrow English words whilst at the same time inserting a vowel before the word, so that an English word like *snob* becomes *esnob* in Spanish and Turkish. In a word like *station* you put a vowel between /s/ and /t/. So the case to look for would be where one could show, for example, that there is a rule which changes a cluster like /sk/ into /esk/, but there is no rule that changes /sl/ into /sVl/.

Drawing some conclusions from the evidence we have looked at, it seems that although form may follow function to a certain extent, it must do so within certain definable limits. Sure, the reason why you borrow words is functional, but in borrowing these words you must meet the requirements or laws of form. They have their own life in some sense, although, I repeat, form may follow function to a certain extent. That's partly what I tried to capture by saying if you have a language which has prothesis then it must necessarily have epenthesis. If that's true, then this type of general conclusion would follow. Also it would follow that to the extent that it does, i.e., that form has its own laws, it is exactly the extent to which functionally based study of language in its social context is bound to be misleading, in the sense that if the laws of phonology have their own life, then those laws cannot be taken liberties with. They must be respected because they are part of the design of human language. A meaningful study of language in its social context must be a study of the interplay between those laws of our nature which show up as laws of forms.

What I have tried to illustrate here are some laws of phonology. I am taking phonology to be merely one particular instance of the laws of form. These laws of form, of rhythm (weak, strong; less sonorous, more sonorous), are obviously related to questions of rhythm and to the laws that show up as laws of our sociality. The interaction between these two is what must constitute the study of language in its social context. The point that I am trying to make is that irrespective of what functional considerations are involved, irrespective of who needs what, there are certain things one cannot do. These potentialities, laws to the extent they are verifiable, are perhaps the immutable laws of phonological form. Unless we first handle these aspects, we cannot merely go on listing examples of what has been borrowed from which language into which other language.

To take what I have just said to its logical conclusion, ignoring the laws of form may lead to somewhat absurd claims like the claim that there are acts of identity but there is no such thing as language. Ignoring the latter (social aspect) can lead to the equally absurd claim that our sociality cannot play with our linguisticality.

Basically what we want to do in the study of contact phonology, or the study of sociolinguistic aspects of language contact, is to find out what the laws of form are and then proceed to examine what social needs can modify which laws within what limits.

5. LANGUAGE-CONTACT—II: *Lexis and Morphology*

Sociolinguistics resists all illusions of unity which stem from the spirit of grammar.

P. Dasgupta 1993: 53

The last lecture was an attempt to show you why we do things the way we do. The general picture that should emerge should be something like this: if you look at phonological adaptations, then it is essentially a kind of play amongst three things. Basically what seems to be involved in phonological adaptations are the functional, social needs that require that you borrow or adapt certain words from another language. Then there is the intervening dimension of universal phonology, which may be said to contain things like a universal syllabic template and a sonority hierarchy which tell you how the segments in the word that you want to adapt or want to borrow are to be optimally syllabified. Another factor that is involved in the processes of adaptation is that of the phonology of the language that is doing the adaptation.

Let me summarise the picture again. Any study of phonological adaptations of words taken from another language must simultaneously look at three dimensions. Sure, it must look at the functional, social needs. But it must also look at universal phonology and at the phonology of the particular host language.

What I want to talk about here is essentially the matter of lexical borrowing, not looking at the phonological shapes but looking at words as they are, either adopted or borrowed into another language, and some morphological matters.

We begin with lexical matters. Lexical situations of borrowing can be summarized as follows. One can say that anything can be borrowed from one language into another. That's one possible hypothesis, typically associated with the functional view of language. In its extreme form, it in fact says something like this: that given a language contact situation, one can borrow anything if one needs to. Another hypothesis, a formalist one, says that members of some grammatical categories, typically things like conjunctions, cannot be borrowed, ever. These are two extreme positions that no sensible linguist really subscribes to fully, but these are the views implicit in many discussions of language borrowing.

If you look at the facts of the matter that I'll not provide the statistical details for, what seems to be the case is summarized below (where "⊃" represents an implicational relation):

(1) SPACE

$$V \supset A \supset N$$

TIME

I'll paraphrase it for you. If a language has borrowed verbs, then it has necessarily borrowed adjectives. If a language has borrowed adjectives from another language, then it has necessarily borrowed nouns.

If you reconsider the two extreme positions, summarized above, they can be reduced to a more reasonable statement in the form of an implicational law of the sort given above.

As far as borrowing the morphology is concerned, some initial reasonability can be captured by statements like the following (where L stands for full words, D for derivational morphemes and I for inflectional morphemes):

(2) SPACE

$$L \supset D \supset I$$

TIME

(2) above says: if a language has borrowed some inflectional material (that's what I mean by I), then it has necessarily borrowed some derivational material. If a language has borrowed an inflectional suffix from another language, then it must necessarily have borrowed a derivational suffix. And if a language has borrowed some derivational material from another language, then it necessarily has borrowed full words.

Notice I have boxed these hierarchies along the dimension of space and along the dimension of time. What that means is that if you look at the history of any one language, then you'll find similar things. Let's look at English. If English in the year 1413 could be said to have borrowed some verbs from French, then one would necessarily find it to be true that at that time. It actually had already borrowed some adjectives. That's what I mean by the dimension of time.

So, if you look at the history of any one particular language, it follows the same laws that can be articulated in terms of space. If you look at different languages, then they'll show this kind of behaviour. There are lots of languages which have borrowed only nouns from other languages and there are lots of languages that have borrowed nouns and adjectives. Two that come to mind immediately are Hindi (spoken in India) and Japanese. Japanese has borrowed nouns and adjectives, just like Hindi. But neither in Hindi nor in Japanese is it possible to borrow verbs. There are specific reasons as to why verbs cannot be borrowed by Japanese or Hindi. There is no need to go into those reasons here. The idea is that languages seem to obey a general disposition or a general law of the kind that can be summarized as an implicational scale that you have already seen.

It seems that a reasonable approach to take to language borrowing is to reject both of the extreme functionalist and formalist positions. The former, I remind you, typically takes the stance that anything can be borrowed if appropriate conditions of contact are present. The latter says that there are certain things that can never be borrowed. Both of these statements seem to be empirically unjustifiable. What we need to say is something of the sort the two borrowing hierarchies in fact say.

Let us look in detail at some specific morphological cases that will give concrete substance to what I am talking about. Consider the so-called redundant compounds, exemplified in (3), that Hindi came up with somewhere around the 15th century:

(3) (a) *tan* - *badan*
+Native -Native
body body
'body etc.'

(b) *vivah* - *šadi*
+Native -Native
marriage marriage
'marriage etc.'

(c) *dhan* - *daulat*
+Native -Native
money money
'money etc.'

(d) *šak* - *sabji*
+Native -Native
vegetable vegetable
'vegetable etc.'

These compounds have some rather peculiar properties. One of them is, as you can see through the glosses that I have provided, that both parts of the word mean the same thing; so the word *tan* means 'body' and the word *badan* means 'body'. Or, to take example (c), the first word *dhan* means 'money' and the second word *daulat* also means 'money' or 'wealth'.

The second structural property they have is that the first word is invariably of native origin (it comes from native lexical stock) and the second word is invariably of Perso-Arabic origin in most cases. Generally, the pattern is that the first word is from Sanskrit (the native stock) and the second is either of Persian origin or Arabic origin (borrowed into Hindi via Persian).

How are we to explain these compounds? Let us agree to call them 'redundant compounds' for the sake of convenience. Let's take the third example, *wealth*, that means 'gold property, shares, stocks, jewellery etc.' i.e., the entire range of things from which you could derive wealth. It is a very general term, which comes from the whole range of things which could be associated with money or wealth. How is its genesis to be explained? How did it come about in the language?

There are various possibilities. One possible explanation for their genesis would that the examples like (a)-(d) are the results of language contact (Kachru 1980). The genesis of these compounds can, in other words, be explained in functional terms of Hindi having been in contact with Persian roughly from 1011 to 1513.

Suppose that this explanation is true. It raises two questions: Will contact always give rise to things like (3a-d)? If you have a contact situation, would you always come up with compounds of this kind? If not, how is the difference between situations when it does and when it does not to be explained? There are, obviously, two logical possibilities. (a) Every time there is linguistic contact between two languages, such compounds will come into existence. (b) Sometimes they will and sometimes they will not. If the second possibility turns out to be true, one would have to explain why in certain cases compounds of this kind come into existence and in certain other cases they don't.

Now, consider some interesting facts that might help us decide between various alternative explanations of this. Notice that contact between English and French lasted roughly about the same amount of time as between Hindi and Persian. Despite that, in English you do not say things like **weather-climate*; neither do you say things like **climate-weather*. In this case, one item is of Latin or Romance origin and the other is of non-Romance origin. You can't combine these two. There are only a handful of cases of this type. You can perhaps add one more word

— *oak tree*. *Oak* is old Germanic for *tree* — that will be comparable to Hindi. *Maid servant* is another possible example of a redundant compound in English; *maid* implies the sense of being a servant. Another example is *door port* (the little door inside the door from which you let your cat or dog out). That's about the extent of combinations in which the first word is from English and the second clearly from Romance.

Also compare the Hindi-Persian contact with French English contact, which has been taking place in contemporary Quebec, Canada. Interestingly, there are no examples, although the intensity of contact between English and French in England and between French and English in Quebec, Canada is roughly comparable to the contact situation between Persian and Hindi.

Despite this, one finds that in the Hindi case there are lots of compounds like this, but in the French-English and English-French contact situations there aren't any. But more important is the fact that in Hindi it is a very productive rule. You can make up such compounds even though they don't appear in a dictionary. Any competent speaker who controls the two lexicons of the language can come up with compounds like these.

How does this kind of thing come about? Consider the following responses to that question: (a) We don't know. (b) The two contact situations must have been different. If you take the functionalist view, which says that whatever happens in a situation of language contact is to be decided exclusively in terms of social functional needs, if you take that position you'll be forced to go along with the second response, i.e. that the two contact situations must have been different.

Suppose you actually do take the view that the difference is the result of the fact that the two contact situations must have been different. In doing so, you are commiting yourself to the view that contact situations vary from each other *ad infinitum*. So that if you say that the difference between the contact situations between Hindi and Persian and between English and French on the one hand, and between French and English on the other, are different, then you are logically committing yourself to the view that the number of differences in contact situations must be infinite. No two contact situations are the same. This is the kind of positions one would be forced into if one were to take the position that it is the functional social needs of the community that decide what is to be done and how new forms are or are not created.

Now, consider some further facts of Hindi. It has some interesting features independently of its Persian contact. It has words like the following:

(4) (a) *dane - dane*
grain grain
'each grain'

(b) *kadam - kadam*
step step
'each step'

(c) *šahar - šahar*
city city
'each city'

Both words are from the native stock in (a) but from the non-native stock in (c). No contact is involved. You can take a word and repeat it. If you do repeat it, you get a distributive reading. If you say *grain*, you mean 'grain' but if you say *grain-grain*, then you mean 'each grain'. The universal quantifier is expressed in this language by repeating the word. In English, one says *each grain*.

Another interesting fact about Hindi is that it also allows one to repeat or reduplicate part of a word in order to create the reading "etc". So if I want to talk about bread, soup etc, one way to talk about them is to take the word *roti* 'bread' and conjoin it with *roti*. Or, to take another example, *namak* ('salt') becomes *namak-vamak*. That means 'salt, pepper and pickle', whatever you associate with a meal.

This pattern is a very productive one, though there is no contact involved. Another pattern in the language is exemplified as in (5) below:

(5) (a) *kəm - jyada*
less more
'more or less'

(b) *unča - niča*
high low
'high or low'

(c) *amir - garib*
rich poor
'rich and poor' (everybody)

If you want to say something like more or less, which in English is a phrase, what you do is to take the first word *kəm* ('less') and the other *jyada* ('more');, you put the two together and you come up with a new word. This new word *kəm-jyada* is equivalent to the English phrase *more or less*. Another example will be: take the word for 'high' and the word for 'low' and put them together. You have a new word — equivalent to the English phrase *high and low*. Or, if you want to talk about everybody that including the rich and the poor, in English, you'll have to say *rich and poor*, but in Hindi — and again these examples are crucial to establishing the fact that it has nothing to do with contact — you take the word for "rich" and the word for "poor" and put them together to mean "everybody".

Given the existence of these patterns, it is a very minor extension of the rules of reduplication of Hindi that makes it possible for the language to come up with words like (3a-c). These patterns taken together give you a set of re-duplication rules in the language, and all that one is doing in order to come up with compound nouns like (3a-c) is simply extending what is already possible in the language.

In particular, given words of the type exemplified in (5) which have the property that if you take an adjective and its antonym, you come up with a new word; or if you take a word and its synonym, you come up with a new word. This means that the grammatical potential of this language already contains the potentiality or possibility of constructing compounds like (3a-c).

Suppose we take this view seriously. Now it becomes trivial to explain that facts like this do not obtain in the English-French contact situation or the French-English contact situation. That is because neither Romance nor Germanic have this sort of reduplication. So it does not really matter how long the contact was, or how many speakers there were or there were not. What really matters is the systematic exploitation of processes of reduplication that have been available to the grammar of Indic languages since about the 12th century B.C. These have not been available to either Germanic or Romance. The reason that these kinds of compounds are not possible in English has nothing to do with differences in the contact situations. It has something to do with the fact that grammatically the potential is not there. Even if the contact situation between English and French was exactly like the contact situation between Hindi and Persian, Turkish, or Arabic in Northwest India, it would not be necessary to invoke the explanation which says these two situations must have been different by definition.

The point I am trying to make is that even if these two situations were identical, the prediction is that this kind of construction, the redundant compound, will never arise on Germanic grounds. What seems to be going on in general terms can be summarized, roughly, as: the Hindi-Persian contact situation shows that it is possible for a language to extend itself in certain ways, if it has the potential to do so.

This kind of creativity is very different from what is commonly called interference, or modification, or adaptation creativity. What is going on here is very different from interference guided modifications that later get institutionalized as adaptations or forms which are incorporated. What is going on here, in the case of redundant compounds, is that these things demonstrate quite clearly a very unambiguous case of genuine bilingual creativity. What you are doing is not merely adapting things; under the contact situation you are exploiting your own potential to its fullest, not by modifying words from another language, but by extending your own system in an entirely logical, natural way.

If this interpretation is valid, what is going on in the lexicon and morphology can be summarized as follows: Given new social functional needs, what you find, repeatedly, is that when some languages come in contact with other languages, then one of the natural ways in which they cope with the new needs which arise, as a result of this new contact situation, is to extend their inherent potential along the lines of development already available to them in their grammars. These things arise, not because of contact but, because contact creates the need to do them; and the actual way in which this need is met is to use the inherent potential of the grammar that is trying to cope with these things and the fact that there is something external to cope with.

It is not surprising that the evidence from phonological and morphological adaptation (extension) looks pretty isomorphous, if not identical. The general conclusion that I'd like to draw from this is that contact studies, of phonology, or lexical or morphological matters, must systematically and simultaneously pay attention to at least three things. They must pay attention not only to social needs, but also to the disposition of Universal Grammar and inherent guiding principles of each particular grammar that is involved in the contact situation.

6. CODE-MIXING AND CODE-SWITCHING

I take this reasoning to be open to inversion.

H. Boeschoten 1991: 95

The subject of contact can be approached, as we have seen, from two distinct, though complementary, points of view. Whereas the first point of view regards language as an institutional network that concerns itself with varying demands of context and acts as the primary channel of cultural transmission, the second regards it as a system of rules that relates sounds to meanings, the two arbitrary poles that lose their arbitrariness precisely because the system of rules that relates them is shared by the entire speech-community. Language contact and conflict can be studied from either of these points of view. Most studies of language-contact, particularly language-contact in Asia, do not examine grammatical aspects in any detail. They assume some version of what might be called the non-autonomy thesis, defended by, for example, Kachru 1980, and often fail to appreciate the role played by the grammars involved. My hypothesis, as you know by now, is that a contact-description that does not provide a full account of the role of Universal Grammar and of the particular grammars involved is more likely to be not only incomplete, but also inaccurate, if not misleading.

The sociolinguistically or psychologically oriented studies of such processes fail because they do not seem to be able to separate the structural from the non-structural, either because they do not know how, or because they assume some version of the non-autonomy thesis. According to this thesis, the "non" I am talking about is impossible in principle. Some advocates of the non-autonomy thesis would claim that it is necessarily so because grammar is simply a reflection of functional variables of communication. It is, unfortunately, not common for studies dealing with code-mixing to cook up all sorts of word-salads and then proceed to draw all sorts of allegedly psycholinguistic conclusions regarding bilingualism. I would like to argue that unless structural conditions are taken into account, no psycholinguistic conclusions can be drawn that would have any bearing on the nature and structure of the human language faculty. As far as functionalist sociolinguistic studies of such processes are concerned, they seem to be based on a set of assumptions for which no substantive evidence exists. It is easy to say that language is communication, but, I believe, impossible to demonstrate that crucial formal properties of language are straightforwardly related to its communicative function (cf. Chomsky 1980).

In this lecture, I would like to look at code-mixing, a form of linguistic behaviour which produces utterances consisting of elements taken from the lexicons of two different languages. As far as the speakers of a mixed-code are concerned, the alternation between the elements from different lexicons is quite automatic. The process in question goes much beyond inter-sentential code-switching, typically observed in diglossia-type situations in which questions of who speaks what to whom and when seem relevant.

One can study code-mixing from various points of view. One can probe why a bilingual is likely to switch between languages, and ask what brain mechanisms are responsible for the switching. One can even claim that code-switching has something to do with code-répertoires and their functional place within a larger theory of communicative competence and language-in-context. All these studies show something useful and interesting. However, they seem unable to explain why mixed-codes are generally constrained the way they are. As a matter of fact, most such studies implicitly adopt the point of view that there are no structural constraints on code-mixing, at least none that cannot be broken, given the appropriate combination of participants, topic of conversation, intentions, and the like. The problem is, as Pfaff (1976 and 1979), Kachru (1978 and 1980), Joshi (1985), Singh (1981) and others have shown, there clearly are some and, as Singh (1981) argues, no combination of sociolinguistic variables seems strong enough to break them. The question, in other words, is not whether there are any structural constraints but what is the best way to characterize them and whether they can be made to follow from some independently motivated general principle. Although there are several proposals in the contemporary literature that attempt to come to terms with this problem (cf. Sankoff and Poplack 1981, Joshi 1985 and Myers-Scotton 1990), they are all inadequate, including my own (cf. Singh 1985b and DiSciullo, Muysken and Singh 1986).

Be that as it may. What I now find most interesting about the subject is the fact that contemporary research on code-mixing invariably ends up raising questions of bilingual proficiency. Consider, for example, the fact that even Grosjean (1991: 255), whose 1982 classic takes a very liberal position on bilingualism, felt obliged to ask Hyltenstam at the end of the presentation of Hyltenstam (1990) the following question: "When it is mentioned that the patients violated the Equivalence Constraint, could this not be due not so much to their demented speech, but simply to their less proficient Swedish?... How do linguistic constraints fare when one of the languages is not mastered very well?" Both the particular and the general problem raised by Grosjean underline the inevitability of questions of proficiency creeping back into places they had been *ex cathedra* pushed out of.

I take this reasoning, to use a memorable expression of Boeschoten's (1991: 95), "to be open to inversion." The inversion Boeschoten recommands will show that patterns of code-mixing are better seen as evidence for proficiency. The strategy of assuming universal proficiency can only lead to what might be called Grosjean's Problem. We must not assume proficiency and then study code-switching and mixing; we must study switching and mixing to find out about language proficiency. Far too much contemporary research on bilingual behaviour takes far too liberal a view of bilingual proficiency, or so it seems.

That observation allows me to go back to my claim of the late seventies that in the Indian context the people I thought had that balance didn't switch very often. One could sum up the situation aphoristically: "A strong bilingual switches only when he wants to and a weak one when he has to." One obvious interpretation of this aphorism is that whereas the balanced bilingual switches only for non-grammatical reasons, the weak bilingual switches for reasons of both grammatical competence and functional needs. Non-grammatical contingencies — moving in two worlds and indulging in linguistic play — can, it seems, be largely met with just switching.

My proposal may strike one as somewhat biased towards what one might call multilingual puritanism, and I am certainly not prepared to be as liberal about it as, for example, Grosjean (1982). I am actually not even convinced that the thunder, as Hymes has repeatedly argued, has entirely gone out of Bloomfield's White Thunder. Non-exposure to certain domains in the case of the monolingual speaker may, after all, be the analogue of the non-use of a language in certain domains in the case of the bilingual speaker.

Let me explore the idea that we ought to study patterns of code-mixing in order to find out if we can indeed speak of bilingualism rather than get bogged down by constraints and their violations. I should perhaps begin with Poplack (1980), who suggested that there WAS a correlation between patterns of mixing and bilingual proficiency.

Her hypothesis regarding that correlation has many parts, some of which are reproduced in (1) below:

(1) (i) Code-switching, then, rather than representing deviant behaviour, is actually a suggestive indicator of degree of bilingual competence (p. 616)

(ii) The cline of bilingualism follows the percentage of intrasentential switches (59% for " true bilinguals")

(iii) Expanding bilingual grammars can be represented as follows:

(iv)

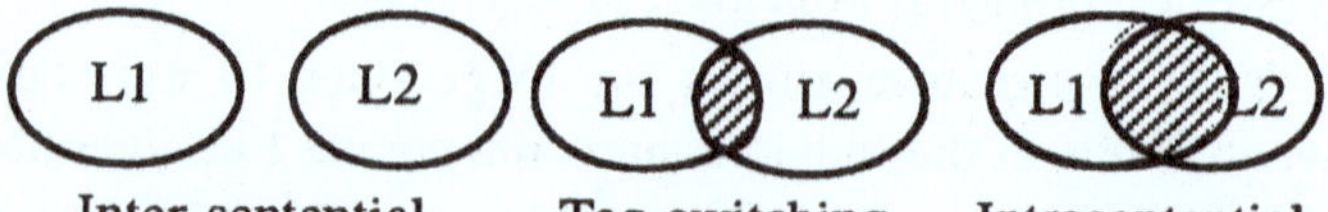

Inter-sentential swiching — Tag-switching — Intrasentential switching

I do not mean to quibble, but it is difficult to refrain from noting that

I do not mean to quibble, but it is difficult to refrain from noting that the set of non-overlapping figures above "intersentential switching" does not prohibit the interpretation that if you do know the two languages only separately, you are not a bilingual, because you don't have any intersection and the last possible figure in this series will spell not the death of two languages but the birth of true bilingualism. It may actually, as Bakker sensitively and tellingly shows, announce the birth of a new language, but I shall return to this later. Perhaps the difficulties presented by Poplack's pictures are inherent to the metalanguage she employs. Despite its caveats regarding nominal, non-parametric, ordinal, and knock-outs, the metalanguage she uses is known to do well only in the middle ranges (cf. Rao 1992).

My own observations, the full details of which I must reserve for a longer piece, add up to a picture apparently at odds with the one presented by Poplack and some others. Speakers I would classify as "true bilinguals" do not generally code-mix at all; and when they do in order to accomodate those they consider to be their country cousins, they stop at parentheticals, mostly things like *aččʰa* 'o.k.', and *hã̄* 'yes'. They do, however, indulge in what I call special switches, switches that require accessing their two grammars in very skillful ways. They come in two varieties. The first one is illustrated in (10) below:

(2) (i) *Dhanyvad... or yeh angrezwala dhanyavād nahin hé*
Thank you and it English thank you not is
'Thank you and it is not an English 'thank you''.

(ii) *Acha bhai, jese urdu me kahate he bona pati.*
Well, now, as Urdu in said bon appétit
'Well, as we say in Urdu, 'bon appétit''.

The second variety of special switches, the invisible one, is hard to illustrate without going into a detailed discussion of syntactic matters, but it is easy to point to. Any one who has ever read Achebe, Raja Rao, or Rushdie would know how the boundaries of what we call English can be gently and entirely legitimately pushed in the direction of African topicalization, Sanskrit *tatpurusha* compounds, or Urdu semi-free word-order. These switches remain invisible to the ordinary eye and inaudible to the ordinary ear and constitute the true bilingual's revenge on interference enthusiasts.

The speakers that I would classify as "apparently bilingual" do the sorts of things that fly in the face of "government" , "equivalence" morpheme and functional head constraint, and anything else one can think of. They are quite like Bakker's Michif speakers. The reason that Pandit was able to find counter-examples to every constraint ever proposed is because her population was made up of a bunch of metropolitan teenagers unable to use either Hindi or English beyond a few seconds. Theirs is a language that is, in the words of Adorno (1992: 291) "not open to any calculus", a language that "arises only in pieces and out of the disintegration of the existing languages".

Similar considerations MAY apply to the Maori-English morphological grasshopping from which Eliasson (1990 and 1991) gets his violations of the Free Morpheme Constraint. The violations of the Free Morpheme Constraints, in other words, may spell trouble for Poplack as well as attrition, a possibility actually suggested by Eliasson (1990), though he feels that Eruera's 1975 informant provides evidence for word-internal switches in highly accomplished bilingual speakers. My experience tells me that although the Free Morpheme Constraint is violable, even reasonably competent bilinguals do not violate this admittedly doubly redundant constraint — doubly redundant because, as Eliasson (1991) shows, it trivially follows from what might be called lexical integrity and because of Giesbers' (1989) razor.

I'd like to join Eliasson in his plea for a more thorough examination of interference, something almost invariably interpreted in a unidirectional way. If such switches were indeed examples of "creative and skilled utilization of the structural resources of two languages", one would expect intraword switches in both directions. In North-India, this is certainly not the case, and I am not fully convinced that such examples as have been gleaned from the Maori-English context exemplify creative and skillful utilization of the structural resources of TWO languages. English morphology is certainly not used by the speakers who say /šapã/ and /termõ/ for *shops* and *terms* to show their bilingual skills in the

Indian context, and the unidirectionality of such switches in the Maori case is no less striking.

As far as Adorno's sensitive — the arrogant amongst us will say "pre-theoretical" — characterization is concerned, consider the following observation by Pandit (1986: 29):

(3) This is where lies the crux of the problem. There are difficulties in arriving at the system of MHE [Mixed Hindi English] because unlike the languages it comprises it does not have any "native-speakers". It has only "users" as distinct from "native-speakers"...

Despite her confusion at the possiblity of the apparent birth of a new language, she is able to capture both the disintegration and the defeat of the calculus, albeit clumsily. I say confusion because ethnographically she goes out of her way to show that MHE is in fact an emerging new code and yet she insists on a literal interpretation of the epithet "mixed" in the name she gives this code. She is a bit like us all when we talk about borrowed words. The Varanasi taxi-driver's answer to Hock: /a:p universiti jā̃ẽge, pahale kyõ nahī̃ kaha/ — he had first used the High Hindi word *vishwavidyalay* for university — should serve as a warning to us all.

She does, however, later indicate that her MHE may have rules of its own, providing part of the answer demanded by the status of hybrid forms, illuminatingly discussed in Eliasson (1990). Bhatia (1989) provides further evidence for the fact that Pandit's MHE does in fact have rules that belong neither to English nor to Hindi. It exhibits, for example, a special process of deriving the infinitival verb forms from nouns and verbs which is taken neither from English nor from Hindi.

People in the middle range of bilingual competence, obviously, do the sort of things Kachru (1978), Bhatt (1994), and I (cf. Singh 1985, for example) have reported on — viz, mostly code-switching but also some intrasentential mixing. The switching is generally governed by topics and the mixing by the sorts of considerations Poplack and Muysken have brought to our attention.

One is, obviously, entitled to know what the objective correlates of my labels such as "true bilingual " and "apparent bilingual" are. The diagram below lists some of them.

(4)

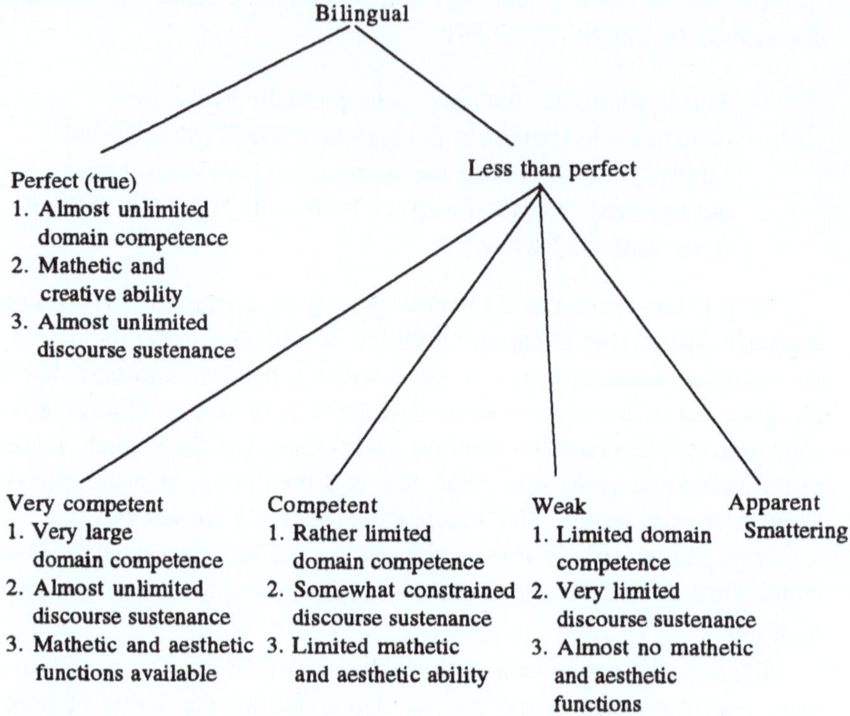

The taxonomy given in (4) may not work, Backus (1993) suggests, because of "the question of norms". Apparently, what he has in mind is a community's ability to set its own norms. The relativization implied by Backus will, I am afraid, makes it impossible to compare one bilingual community with another, at least in terms of proficiency. On this view, Butler English in the India of 19th century is as much an instance of bilingualism as Standard Indian English in contemporary India and the smattering of German handled by the community of tourist-guides in Varanasi India is as much an instance of bilingualism as the Dutch-Turkish bilingualism of Backus' Hilversum girls. It is interesting to note that despite the difficulties, Backus himself has to use locutions such as "in much the same way as any native speaker does" and "characteristic of native speakers."

What is at stake is essentially "what does it take to count as a native speaker of a language?" The only formal answer I have ever been able to come up with is: a native speaker of a language is a speaker who shares relatively stable grammticality judgements on utterances said to be from his language with other speakers. Notice that the need to play the grammaticality game arises only when the pragmatic function is supplemented by the mathetic and aesthetic functions.

The definition given above excludes, in my view, not only the tourist guides of Varanasi but also Pandit's undergraduates who have remarkably inconsistent judgements on utterances in both Hindi and English. Besides, the latter don't really ever use either language exclusively. Again, I am not aware of any mathetic or creative activity in German in Varanasi or in Hindi or in English amongst Pandit's undergraduates. They seem to be poised at the brink of a possible monolingualism.

Be that as it may, the point is that both monolingual and bilingual proficiency IS measurable across communities despite differences in norms because these cannot alter what it takes to count as a speaker. If your community requires you to do only this or that with L_i or L_j, you may count as a pragmatic user of L_i or L_j within and outside that community, but "He knows some French" is not the same thing as "He knows French".

So, if the resolution of the apparent contradictions in the results of Backus, Bentahilla and Davies, and Singh on the one hand and Pfaff (1976, 1979), Poplack and Nortier on the other is not to be found in the infinite multiplicity of highly relativized individual "bilingual settings", what options do we have? Two, I'd say: (1) one of these groups of researchers is wrong and (2) they are both right for different ranges of bilingual proficiency.

I think the second option is the right one. Let me explain why. Poplack's work, for example, is to be situated within the context of combating unwarranted allegations against non-upper class Puerto-Ricans. It is worth remembering that "decay" and "deviant behaviour" provide the constant counterpoint to her defence of the bilingual ability of her informants. Mine, on the other hand, deals with hightly educated upper class metropolitan Indians. My informants have never been subjected to such criticism. If anything, they have used such criticisms against, for example, Pandit's "lost generation". My true bilinguals must count as native speakers of Hindi and English, though I am not sure if Poplack's or Pandit's can count as native-speakers of the two languages attributed to them.

The claim that my true bilinguals must count as native speakers of English and Hindi is supported by (1) their ability to use either language exclusively in almost any domain or register for hours at a time and (2) their habitual use of them for mathetic and creative functions (cf. Prabhu 1989).

Since there is some debate, created mostly by the TESL industry in Britain and the United States, about the existence of such speakers, let me clarify a few things. The absurdity of the TESL-industry inspired paraoxical claim, that although Indian English is a variety of English, IE speakers are not native-speakers of English should be obvious. Although it makes sense to say that a speaker of variety $_i$ of language L is not a speaker of variety $_j$ of that language, it makes no sense to say that although $_i$ is a variety of L, speakers of $_i$ are not speakers of L.

Suppose it is possible to establish what it takes to count as a speaker. Now, the question of relativization of norms can be handled straightforwardly. Once Americans, Englishmen, Canadians, Indians, and Singaporeans are counted in, we can of course talk about American, Canadian, or Singaporean English. The fact that some of us don't count some of these in has to do with the extralinguistic fact that they don't own enough shares in the stock called English and nothing whatsoever to do with any linguistic criteria I'm aware of (cf. Singh 1994, Singh *et al,* 1995, and, to anticipate a bit, Lecture 9). As opposed to speakers of Indian English, who live in an endo-normative context, the transplanted communities studied by Backus, Nortier and Poplack live in a doubly exo-normative context: the norms of both the languages they are supposed to be speakers of reside outside these communities. There is, to the best of my knowledge, no Turkish-Dutch or Dutch-Turkish yet.

As far as my "less than perfect bilinguals" are concerned, they clearly don't have anything like native or near-native competence in English, the first sub-type — "very competent bilinguals" — being an intermediate case. Whereas my 1992 paper drew its data from conversations and elicitations from the group labelled "Perfect Bilinguals", my earlier work was based on data from this intermediate group. I had never worked with "Weak" or "Apparent Bilingual" speakers till last year.

Whereas the code/mixing behaviour of my first and second group of informants suggests that the perfect bilinguals do not indulge much in it and the very competent ones indulge only in inter-discourse/sentential switching and reasonably smooth intrasentential mixing, the work of other researchers such as Bhatia and Pandit (1986) suggests that some so-called bilinguals do indulge in rugged switching, constituent insertion, and even intramorphemic switching. I have already argued that independent criteria show that Pandit's informants cannot be counted as speakers of either Hindi or English — in fact, she herself speaks of them as users of M(ixed) H(indi) E(nglish). I have no difficulty in classifying them as "apparent" bilinguals for reasons I have already provided.

The North-Indian situation is, thus, very complex, and invites reflection that goes beyond the construction of a typology of code-mixing communities because within this community itself three subcommunities can be isolated relatively easily — the one that doesn't mix, the one that does, and the one that only appears to. What needs to be constructed is not a typology of code-mixing communities but a methodology for identifying comparable populations across communities because most settings, it seems to me, contain these three types (cf. Backus 1993, again). To construct typologies of the former sort is to abandon the hope of finding the similarities that cut across the differences functionalist categories are bound to hide.

Let me get to the scale of bilingual proficiency. It is given in (5) below:

(5)

High

- Discourse and invisible switches
- Discourse switches
- Speech act switches
- Adjacency pair switches
- Parenthetical switches
- Intrasentential switches

Low

Although (5) above seems essentially correct to me, the lower range clearly needs more work and refinement. The possible challenge from the behaviour of a very weak bilingual speaker who knows that his interlocutor does not know his preferred and dominant language does not, however, constitute a threat to the scale. For reasons of cooperation and communication, such a speaker will use the other's language even if he has only a smattering of it. His accommodative talk may create the impression that he is not switching or mixing at all, leading the analyst to classify him, according to the criteria enshrined in (4), as very proficient in his L_2. This accommodative/cooperative moment can be easily safeguarded against by adding the obvious proviso that when the proficient bilingual switches, his productions are grammatical *vis-à-vis* the language he is using at a given point of time.

How do I reconcile the scale with the facts reported in Poplack, for example? I think the answer is easy. Poplack is dealing with the middle and lower ranges where the inability to mix, as opposed to the habit of not mixing, is indeed indicative of the lack of any proficiency in L_2 and the ability to insert only tags is indeed indicative only of rudimentary control of the other language. Her "true bilinguals" are, in other words, the only ones that have any bilingual ability worth writing home about. I do not know what sort of competence in English and Spanish can be attributed to these speakers. The information that Poplack provides is somewhat circumstantial — we know a lot about their age, sex, background, and attitudes, but not much about their ability, for example, to sustain discourses in the two languages in question.

It would not have escaped your attention that there is a sort of flip-flop here — both the perfect bilingual and the almost perfect monolingual do not indulge in any mixing, the former obviously because he can afford not to and the latter equally obviously because he cannot. This is also the case with pause fillers and parentheticals — in the former case, they are put in for Gricean reasons, but in the latter, for entirely linguistic reasons. This flip effect shows that it may not be necessary to go as far as Bentahila and Davies (1992) are willing to go in search for appropriate explanations, though they are certainly right in drawing attention to what they call communicative functions (p. 456).

It has been suggested to me that the differences between Poplack's informants and mine reside not where I think they do but in factors such as social class, education, and metalinguistic awareness. This translation of proficiency to what might loosely be called "class" may be valid, but it must be remembered that in the context in question it straightforwardly implies longer exposure to and proficiency in English. I have, in other words, no objection to adding the noun "class" in conjunction or disjunction with the adjectives 'High' and 'Low' in (5). Neither Backus's upper-middle-class Hilversum girls nor Bentahila and Davies' urbane, upper-class informants could object, because that is where they belong.

As I have no intention of defending the scale in (5) to the last letter — I have not done the work necessary to propose a scale the particulars of which I would want to defend — let me just say that I hope to have persuaded you that such a scale is not only possible but also perhaps necessary, not only to reconcile apparently contradictory results, but also to integrate our findings into some general theory of bilingualism The apparent contradictions we have looked at follow partly from the difficulty of using language to describe linguistic ability and partly from an entirely understandable liberal desire to project partial failure as partial success. An instrumentalist who is as bad at the *sitar* as at the *tabla* is after all quite balanced, and it is this rather unusual sense that the expression "balanced bilingual" seems to have acquired in the current literature. This literature also seems to want to dismiss those who see mixing as evidence of disintegration. In setting linguists up against "intellectuals" — and I hope she was not speaking for us all — all that Poplack (1980:588) may have been able to accomplish is to encourage the interpretation of "a large degree of competence" as "competence" itself. It is, therefore, difficult to see what is meant by saying that code-switching requires more linguistic competence in two languages than is generally assumed. Given that those who bemoan relexification and linguistic disinstegration don't make quantitative statements, the liberal linguist's response is comparable to the assurance that partially skimmed milk contains more fat than is generally assumed. It is not a matter of more or less, but of the fact that now plain, ordinary milk has to be labelled in a marked fashion — *whole milk*. The lax defense offered by some linguists seems to me to be wide of the mark. Even the assurance that a new language may yet be born is a bit like telling a mother whose child is about to die that she is fertile enough to have another one. The solution is, in other words, not to pit linguists against intellectuals but to hope that observation and making sense can proceed together, as they did in the case of Weinreich, even if the sense-making requires some counterfactual idealizations such as his ideal bilingual.

If I could add anything to what Weinreich (1953) said, I would offer that addition as my conclusion. But as I can't — even the scale I am proposing is merely a trivial inference from what he did say — I'll just stop.

7. CROSS-CULTURAL COMMUNICATION

> *We are never locked within a single grammar. Rather, the first grammar that we learn to master already puts us in a position to step out of it and to interpret what is incomprehensible, to assimilate in our own words what at first escapes them.*
>
> J. Habermas 1977: 336

In this lecture, I want to take up the subject of cross-cultural communication, something modern socio-linguistics seems to present as something it can help understand. In order to analyse cross-cultural communication, one can proceed with two entirely different sets of assumptions. These are summarized below under (1):

(1) **Assumptions for analysis of Cross-Cultural Communication**

	(A)	(B)
1.	Linguistic differences cause problems	They only APPEAR to
2.	We are LOCKED	We are actually LIBERATED
3.	Intravariety differences smaller than inter-variety differences	No more, no less
4.	There is miscommunication	There is deafness

5.	The different contexualizing convention (CC) is situated, located, grounded in C2	It is grounded in another part of C1 (the one you're not looking at)
6.	Generally non-repairable	Always repairable
7.	Normative	Non-normative
8.	Assimilative	Cooperative

One can make the assumptions listed on the left (A) or the assumptions listed on the right (B). To begin, we can assume that linguistic differences can and in fact do cause problems of communication, or we can make the opposite assumption that they merely appear to but never have to, unless they are allowed to. The second assumption has to do with L_1. One can assume that if you know a language or if you are a native speaker of a particular variety of a particular language, then you are locked into that variety or locked into that language. The opposite assumption is that knowing a language or knowing a variety, if you think about it, is actually something that liberates you from that language. It appears to lock you in only if you refuse to think about what that language has given you. Third, one can make the assumption that differences that exist between varieties and differences that exist inside each variety are qualitatively different. Or, one can make the opposite assumption that these differences are never either more or less. Fourthly, one can make the assumption that there is miscommunication in situations involving speakers of different varieties. Or, one can make the assumption that there is no miscommunication in the standard sense of the word but that there is only deafness from the other side. Next, one can assume that different contextualising cues that one isolates are situated, located or grounded in the culture where they come from or where they normally get interpreted. Or, alternatively, one can make the opposite assumption that these contextualization cues are generally grounded not in the culture one says that they regularly come from but in that part of one's own culture that one has decided to ignore. It will allow you to think more concretely. If you say that those who do not say "thank you" are not expressing verbal gratitude appropriately enough, the grounding for the relevant contextualizing cue is not in the fact that the other language does not express verbal gratitude this way but in the fact that English has proverbs like "Silence is golden". When one passes that judgement, what one is ignoring is not the other culture, not the other language, but that part of one's own language that, institutionally, one is encouraged to ignore.

One can, of course, assume, as most of these studies do, that what actually takes place is miscommunication, and that we need to understand it. One can, however, make the opposite assumption that what takes place is communication and that it is the analysts who misconstrue that as miscommunication. One can also assume that given the appropriate conditions of charity, rationality, and humanity, all putative cases of miscommunication are in fact repairable.

These assumptions add up to something. And I have tried to show that assumptions (A) seem to me to promote the view that use of language in social context is normative and must be described in normative terms. And that is related to the larger political predicate of assimilation. If you adopt or use certain kinds of cues that are given to you normatively, then your task is to assimilate to those who use those contextualizing cues. If you don't, you are refusing to assimilate. The assumptions (B), on the other hand, add up to the view that may be called non-normative. It does not require compliance with a set of pre-fixed norms and, therefore, leads to a plea for making sense together.

As all of this might sound a little abstract, what I'll do now is to look at a full discourse. We will attempt to analyse it under the two sets of assumptions just outlined. In the discourse reproduced below, NS stands for native speaker and NNS stands for non-native-speaker. This is an encounter in which a student of English as a foreign language has been asked to call a television shop in the United States to find out what the cost of a new television might be. This discourse is a transcription of a conversation between this foreign student (NNS) and a sales lady, who is an NS.

NS: Hello
NNS: Hello. Could you tell me about the price and size of Sylvania color TV?
NS: Pardon?
NNS: Could you tell me about the price and size of Sylvania TV...color?
NS: What did you want? A service call?
NNS: —seventeen inch—
NNS: Humh?
NS: What did you want? A service call, or how much to repair a TV?
NNS: Yeah. Eh TV color.
NS: Seventeen inch?
NNS: O.K.
NS: (*pause*) Well is it a portable?
NNS: m hm.
NS: What make is it? (*pause*) What is the brand name of the TV?
NNS: Ah, Sony please.
NS: We don't work on Sony's.
NNS: —sss—
NNS: Or Sylvania. [low /a/]
NS: Sylvania? [/ei/]
NNS: un humh.
NS: Uh Sylvania, O.K., that's American made.
NNS: — uh humh —
NNS: O.K.
NS: All right. Uhh, portables have to be brought in.
NNS: m hm
NS: And there's no way I can tell you how much it'll cost until he looks at it.
NNS: m hm
NS: And it's a twelve fifty deposit.
NNS: O.K.
NS: And if he can fix it, that applies to labor, and if he can't he keeps the twelve fifty for his time and effort.
NNS: (*slight pause*) m hm

NS: How old of a TV is it? Do you know off hand?
NNS: O.K. Nineteen inch?
NS: How old of a TV is it? Is it a very old one or only a couple years old.
NNS: Oooooh. So-so (*long pause*) Umm, about how old?
NS: The only thing you can do is bring it in, you know, and let him look at it 'n go from there.
NNS: (*long pause*) New television please. (*clears throat*)
NS: Oh, you wanna know (*long pause*) how much a new television is?
NNS: Yeah, I wan' buy one please.
NS: (*pause*) Do we wanna buy one?
NNS: uh humh
NS: (*long pause*) Is it a Sylvania?
NNS: Sylvania TV color.
NS: (*long pause*) Well, even you know even if we buy 'em we don't — we don't give much more 'n twenty five dollars for 'em. Cause time we fix 'em up and resell 'm we can't get more 'n —
NNS: m hm
NS: —hundred dollars out of 'em time we put our time 'n parts in it.
NNS: Is it the ... seventeen inch?
NS: (*long pause*) Well I'd—you know the only thing I can tell you to do is you'd have to come to the shop, I'm on the extension at home. The shop's closed.
NNS: m hm. Nineteen inch?...you don't have?
NS: (*short pause*) Do we have a nineteen inch?
NNS: Yeah.
NS: No, I've got a seventeen inch new RCA.
NNS: O.K. Thank you. Bye
NS: m—bye.
NNS: m hm.

Now let us see how it might be analysed. In fact, it has been analysed under assumptions (A). If you look at it under that set of assumptions, you might say things of the sort that Varonis and Gass (1985) do.

Now, look at this discourse and see what is going on. When asked what he wanted in making this telephone call, the NNS responds by saying he wants a 17 inch. This response in normal circumstances could be interpreted as A 17 INCH TELEVISION SET. Varonis and Gass, unfortunately, classify this response as "an inappropriate response." Four lines below that response, when the NNS says again that he is looking for a colour television, that also is identified as an inappropriate response.

Let's continue to look at the discourse under the analysis that has been proposed. If you look at the end of the first page of the transcription, it begins with the NNS, after a long pause, saying "new television please." The line that says "I wanna buy one please" two lines later is analysed as the NNS goal, which, we are told, is different from what has been invoked for him by the NS. Varonis and Gass say that there is something wrong with the NNS saying that because his goal is different from what has been invoked for him by the salesperson. The salesperson has invoked the goal for him that he wants a T.V. repaired. She runs a T.V. repair shop, and she makes the assumption that anyone calling her has a T.V. that needs to be repaired. In that context, these analysts point out that the response "I want buy one" is actually incongruous with the goal he is SUPPOSED to have.

The sentence that follows, these analysts admit, provides evidence that perhaps there is some reason to believe that the NS could have understood what the NNS was trying to say. But, in the words of our analysts "accepting what the NNS said would involve a major change." Therefore, the NNS's goal must be rejected! That's actually what the NS does.

Further down the next line, they point out, the NNS also misunderstands the NS. The NS at one point says that she is on the telephone extension at home and the shop is closed. That is described by these analysts as a very polite "put off", implying that the NS has somehow gotten tired and would, understandably, like the conversation to be terminated.

They say that the NS in this discourse abandoned her goal five times. She is a salesperson in a T.V. shop and her assumption is that anybody calling there must have a T.V. to be repaired. Poor salesperson, she had to revise her goal 5 times! Our analysts further observe that the NS is "extremely co-operative." These are their words. The NNS, on the other hand, is, they observe, "linguistically deficient" and guilty of a rude put off.

What they mean by "a rude put off" is what you see at the end of the discourse. When the sales person says that she in fact has a 17" T.V., the NNS prefers to sign off. Our analysts point out that he could have continued because now he was about to meet his goal: he could have considered the possibility of buying a T.V., something that he was looking for. He decides not to take up that invitation, and instead says "Thank you, Bye." And this "Thank you, Bye" is described by our analysts as a very rude put off.

Now look at this same discourse under the other set of assumption that we talked about, and see what happens. Notice that in lines 2, 4 and 6 from the beginning the NNS announces his goal about as clearly as it is possible to do so. He begins by saying "Could you tell me about the price and size of Sylvania Colour TV" and repeats that just a bit later when he says "Could you tell me about the price and size of Sylvania TV... colour." He begins, as I said before, the discourse with a very clear announcement of what he wants. Now contrast this, for example, with the fact that the analysis under the first approach begins after the first six lines. The analysts have nothing to say about the first five lines of the discourse, the part of the discourse in which the NNS has announced his goal twice. They begin their analysis with the first line that they could plausibly construe as an inappropriate response. The first part is left unexamined, indeed unnoticed.

Despite the clear announcement of the goal and its repetition, the NNS doesn't succeed. Notice the NS sentence "What did you want? A service call?" It is, I would like to argue, the first inappropriate response of the discourse. It makes absolutely no allowance for the goal that the NNS has already announced twice. The first genuinely inappropriate response is, in fact, by the NS. She can ask that question if and only if she has not heard what the NNS has already said more than once.

If you go down two lines in the discourse, she asks the same question again "What did you want?" Notice that given the NNS announcement of his goal, one should ask what is the warrant for asking this question? Why is she asking this question when the NNS has made it absolutely clear that what he is looking for is a colour TV—he has even gone to the extent of specifying the brand name of the TV he wants.

Further down, the NNS hesitates a little but NS refuses to be patient. And every time there is a pregnant pause, she comes in with a line or two, giving the details of the story that will follow from the presuppositions that she is making about why this person is calling.

A bit further down in the discourse one can see clearly that she is not paying attention to what the speaker is saying. Ironically, she is paying enough attention to correct the quality of the vowel used in the pronunciation of the name Sylvania by emphasising the vowel that ought to be used in American English. A bit further down the discourse, she puts in an extra bit of information that they don't work on Sony and that they work only on Sylvania because they are American, as if that really mattered, except for some other point that she wants to make.

So, if you look at the structure of the discourse at the bottom, it looks very strongly like what is going on is that the NS has tremendous difficulty with silence. She is not willing to provide the NNS the time that he needs. She is very impatient. The NNS is being subjected to what I shall call the Henry James regret. When Henry James was close to his death, someone asked him if he had any regrets. He replied "Yes, I wish people hadn't finished my sentences for me." That's apparently what the NS is doing here. Every time the NNS wants to say something, she jumps in and completes the sentence for him.

Let us look a bit more at this discourse. In the middle of it, there are three places where the NNS pauses to try to articulate his response, but invariably the NS jumps in, saying in effect: "Don't even try to talk because I am interrupting." She keeps interrupting with lines which seem ready-made for the kind of story that she wants to tell. It is particularly telling in the case after the first pause, when the NS says that there is no way she can tell him how much it cost until the repair-man looks at it. Now this is a very clear indication that she is very impatient with the speaker. No pauses are permitted.

Notice that if one were to make a charitable interpretation, one could say that what the NNS speaker is doing, for example, where there is a long pause, identified as such by our analysts, is to understand the puzzle as to why all these questions are being asked, for he has made it absolutely clear at the very beginning to what he is after. The word *old* is repeated and his saying that he is looking for 19" is lost in the NNS' obsession of how old the television is. Again it is a very clear indication of the fact that the NS is really deaf, despite the fact that she hears the phonemes clearly enough to be able to correct them.

A bit further down the discourse, you see the continuation of the same problem. It is much later, actually almost towards the end, that she sort of acknowledges "Oh you want to know how much a new T.V. costs?" Now, this is an acknowledgement of a statement that was made at the beginning of the discourse, very late indeed. Even then, as soon as the NNS says "yes I want to buy one please" — third time in fact — the NS ignores it, and the pronoun *I* is interpreted pseudo-cooperatively as *we*: "Do we want to buy one?" And this despite the fact that he has made it very clear that he is the one who wants to buy it. Her continued difficulty with silence escapes the attention of Varonis and Gass. She is not willing to understand what the other person is saying but must supply her own bits of discourse which may not be related to what the NNS is asking for. What is characterized by Varonis and Gass as "a polite put off" is really anything but polite.

Even if we leave the adjectives out, at the end of the discourse one has a very surprising announcement. Despite all the details and detours the NS has been putting in, she actually says that she has got a 17" new R.C.A. for sale, something she could have expressed very, very early in the discourse. When he called to find out if he was in the right place to buy a TV, she could have said that she had a new 17" TV. She could have avoided beating around the repair-shop bush. Now, you can see precisely why; what is characterized under the first approach as a rude put off is actually a very polite signing off because the NNS has repeatedly made very clear what he is looking for and the NS comes up with her surprise announcement only towards the end.

At the end, he says, very politely, "Thank you. Bye" making it clear that he is not interested in a 17" T.V. Why should he be? He was looking for a 19" colour T.V. The conclusion that one is forced to draw from this analysis, done under the second approach, can only be that the NS is almost deaf. Or, equivalently, that she is full of her own presuppositions. Her belief space or her presuppositional space is so full of what she wants to entertain that she is in principle incapable of hearing what the NNS is saying.

Let us further contrast these two analyses, one done under the first set of assumptions and the other done under the second. The first analysis, understandably, puts the burden of "miscommunication" on the NNS. Varonis and Gass suggest repeatedly in their article that the NS is very cooperative and that what is wrong with this discourse, why this discourse misfires, why this discourse creates the difficulties it does, is the fact that the NNS is "linguistically deficient." But I have tried to point out that if you look at it from the other point of view, the one incorporating the assumptions of charitability, humanity and rationality, then you are forced to conclude that the problem is not with the NNS but it is almost exclusively with the NS. The NS is not able to understand what is said because she is predisposed to not understanding, not even trying to understand.

What follows from all this is, I would like to add, that one ought to concentrate on conditions for non-repair. The task, in other words, is not to isolate the contextual cues and discourse strategies. What one should actually be looking for is the set of conditions that makes it impossible for some speakers to repair what has been said. And repair takes place under conditions of humanity, charitability and rationality. These conditions generally are socio-historical and economic in nature. The reason our native speaker is deaf is that the conditions which define her place make her so. The fact that she is not able to repair, even for her own purposes, underlines that the NNS's speech needs no repair as far as he is concerned, but for her own interpretive reasons NS might have repaired them. If she DID NOT, she DID NOT because of conditions of this kind. This leads straight forwardly to some clear methodological recommendations:

(2) Some Methodological Recommendations

Approach 1	Approach 2
(Gumperz, Varonis, Gass, Scarcella, Valentine, etc.)	
Study "miscommunication" to find differences in discourse strategies (DS) and contextualizing conventions (CC)	Study it to find conditions of "non-repair": social, historical, economical
Ignore "Verbal" power	Don't
MAXIMIZE language difference	MINIMIZE it
Assume the lack of equality and proceed as if it didn't matter	Proceed as if nothing other than equality mattered
Take DS's as constituting a valid DOMAIN	Ask for reasons that warrant such a construal
Take discourse to be STRATEGIC	Take discourse to be a participatory search for joint-meaning
Take RATIONALITY to be STRATEGIC (how to get things done)	Take RATIONALITY to be UNABRIDGED

The first approach essentially says that in any analysis of this kind you must ignore whatever power-relations obtain or exist between speakers; the second approach, on the other hand, says don't ignore it, for that will give you some idea of why certain things get misinterpreted. The first approach says one should maximize language differences, so that what happens in the discourse we were looking at can be attributed to the different discourse conventions of Spanish, because the NNS is a native speaker of Spanish the other approach, on the other hand, says that you minimize those differences, implying that there is no need in the case at hand to appeal to the fact that the NNS is a native speaker of Spanish. There is nothing in the discourse that requires that appeal to be launched.

The first approach also says that you assume that the lack of equality among the participants does not really matter; the second approach, on the other hand, says that one should proceed as if NOTHING ELSE really matters. For EFFECTIVE COMMUNICATION to take place, the second approach says, one has to assume that the two speakers engaged in the task of producing a discourse together are operating on the basis of equality and that if factually they are not on an equal footing, then miscommunication is bound to happen, because one of the participants is likely to be deaf.

The first approach says that methodologically the discourse strategies and contextualizing cues of a language constitute a valid autonomous domain of investigation. Although languages can and in fact do differ from each other by the kind of strategies that they employ in constructing discourses, one must, according to the second approach, ask for reasons that warrant such a construal (an autonomous culturalist construal). And that demand follows from the fact that within the same language there are invariably other discourse strategies, other discourse conventions. One must, in other words, justify how these other strategies and conventions can be ignored.

According to the first view, the major methodological recommendation is that you take discourse to be strategic and human rationality to be strategic and analyse discourses with the understanding that they are a matter of getting things done, essentially with the understanding that a discourse is an exercise in power. You talk to the other person not because you want to hear what the other person has to say but because you want the other person to do something for you. That's the only reason for engaging in discourse. The other approach, on the other hand, takes or encourages the assumptions that take discourse as a participatory search for meaning rather than as the locus of one will against the other.

Now you can see how these differences, both in terms of presuppositions and in terms of methodological recommendations, can produce such different kinds of analyses. The first one, I repeat, ends up blaming, fairly extensively, the NNS, and the second one spells out the blame that must be put on NS.

Although the logic of the second interpretation is quite clear, one could quibble and claim that the NS is not solely responsible for what goes wrong. Perhaps the NNS contributed a little bit to this. I have knowingly exaggerated the deafness of the NS because that does seem to me to play a central role in what goes wrong in the communication and because the standard, mainstream analysis absurdly blames only the NNS.

Depending on what one is trying to do, different conclusions naturally follow. If one assumes that the power-determined norms of discourse are the ones that must be followed, one would argue, predictably, that the NNS, or the speaker of the other variety, must follow these norms. I know what the rules of the discourse are, and I'll describe them to the other speaker and he or she must follow them. If he or she does not follow them, the communication will misfire, go wrong. If it does, the blame can easily be attributed to the other speaker. But if one takes the approach that norms are jointly created by both speakers involved in a discourse, other conclusions follow. You cannot say that the norms are to be dictated by anyone. These are continually renewed dynamic processes and arise out of an interaction. But that interaction can take place if and only if both partners are willing to speak and listen at the same time.

The general conclusion would be that any communication in which there is a speaker who only knows how to speak (and not how to hear) or a speaker who only knows how to hear (and is not empowered to speak) is, theoretically, an example of miscommunication.

What is normally described as miscommunication is, in some sense, not miscommunication at all. Putative examples of miscommunication are actually clear examples of precisely how communication has been misunderstood by some analysts. The interaction between speech and silence is completely ignored by them.

Let me try to summarize what it all seems to add up to. Some of the important sociological consequences of the approach that is normally followed in the analysis of cross-cultural communication is that culture is a static, locked-in, objectified thing. Culture is something which is static, solid, unchangeable, a locked-in object, and the task of the other speaker (NNS) is to get hold of this solid object called culture and hold on to it for his dear life. The second sociological consequence of the dominant approach is that the larger symbolic meaning of miscommunication is completely lost. What I mean by larger symbolic meaning of miscommunication is that what is going on in these so called instances of miscommunication is not that the speakers are miscommunicating or misunderstanding each other but that it is the analysts that are misunderstanding the very act. The misunderstanding, in other words, is not in the speaker's but in the analyst's mind.

"Miscommunication" can actually mean a lot of things, depending on society, history, politics, and various other things. It can mean resistance against the centripetal forces, forces that require that you assimilate towards a pre-given, pre-defined norm in which you yourself cannot play any role. That could certainly be one meaning. The other general symbolic meaning of the act of miscommunication ignored by those who analyse miscommunication is that it is actually an invitation to cooperate. Because it is talked about and described as miscommunication, its invitational potential is completely lost. When something like this happens, those who are alleged to be responsible for miscommunication are actually sending out an RSVP, which is not being returned by the analysts. The other speakers, however, understand the message perfectly.

The third sociological consequence of this kind of analysis is very simple. Most anthropologists would acknowledge that what it does is to reduce the other person's culture to ethnicity. Just as contemporary anthropology reduces the others peoples' history to anthropology, this enterprise reduces other cultures to ethnicities. So, it is not an accident, for example, that inter-cultural communication or inter-cultural miscommunication is equally frequently referred to as inter-ethnic communication or inter-ethnic miscommunication. The equivalence between culture and ethnicity is suggestive of the anthropological consequences of this approach. The mainstream analysts reserve the term culture for themselves.

Another necessary social consequence of this approach is that the difference — howsoever it is to be defined, whether in terms of other variety, native, non-native, another ethnicity, whatever the case may be — is excluded from defining the norms of tomorrow. Those who are different will not participate in creating new norms and will have no influence on what the norms of tomorrow look like. Their only task is to learn to live with them.

8. CROSS-SEX COMMUNICATION

> *You know as well as we know that what is just is arrived at in human arguments only when the necessity on both sides is equal, and that the powerful exact what they can, while the weak yield what they must.*
>
> Thucydides, Book V

The discourse-strategies model we looked at in the last lecture has been, perhaps predictably, extended to another domain: cross-sex communication. That is what I want to talk about in this lecture.

In their largely programmatic defense of the Labovian model of diversity, Shapiro and Schiffman (1981) declare the Indian subcontinent open again for "investigation of the kind of phenomena now being done in the West" (176). One of these is cross-sex communication, and the rush is on to universalize the American interactionist's model, sketched out, for example, in Gumperz (1982a, 1982b) and, for the "domain" in question, fleshed out by Maltz and Borker (1982). India has recently been claimed for the model by Valentine (1985, 1986). Her work is a careful attempt to infuse the theories of contemporary interactional sociolinguistics with Indian "empirical content" and deserves a close reading. She applies the currently fashionable strategy model of discourse to the Indian scene and claims to find what the model predicts.

The model in question sees power in structural-functional rather than hierarchical terms. In other words, it sees power as "energy" in successful communication acts. It ignores the uneven distribution of hierarchical power within a society and the contradictions that follow from it and assumes, as Maltz and Borker put it, that problems are not "the result of bad faith" (201), but of differences in the manipulation of discourse strategies. For cross-sex communication, the reasoning of its adherents goes something like this. There are differences in the speaking patterns of American men and women in cross-sex communication. In very general terms, women are "complying and attentive" to their partner's speech, whereas men tend to interrupt the speech of women, challenge their statements, and control the conversation. This necessarily leads to difficulties, which are further exacerbated by stereotypical attitudes.

These researchers believe that such difficulties can be traced back to differences in linguistic socialization and to miscommunication (*à la* Gumperz for interethnic problems). Hierarchical power differentials, the researchers in this paradigm grant, may make some contribution, but overall it is more fruitful to look into the different sociolinguistic subcultures of men and women. They then proceed to describe the "world of boys" and the "world of girls," suggesting that whatever differences there may be in adult speech are merely an extension of what has been learned in childhood. Ostensibly, they stop short of questioning the reason behind such differentiation and leave the distinct impression that one simply cannot fight nature and that in any case it is more interesting to occupy oneself with symptom-analyzing activities (cf. Singh 1984). For further research they generally suggest the investigation of, for example, the speech of tomboys, lesbians and gay men, or the elderly, where, they tell us, power differences have become insignificant.

The second most important characteristic of this model is its almost unqualified acceptance of the transfer of rhetoric hypothesis (see Kaplan 1966 and others). According to this hypothesis, the discourse of non-native speakers is shaped by the discourse conventions and strategies of their native language, usually to their detriment in the native context. It is this unmistakable nonnative color of their discourses and their L1-conditioned mind that make it difficult or impossible for them to master the strategies of the native speaker that cause problems. Not much else is involved, not even principles of communicative cooperation (cf. Varonis & Gass 1985).

By looking at the victims of the politics of power as willing participants, the advocates of this model show precisely how much persuasive power politics can have — certainly enough to be considered one of two major problems of knowledge, Plato's problem and Orwell's problem, as Chomsky (1986) calls them. And there is certainly enough to persuade "researchers" to ignore what is visibly there in their own writings. Valentine provides an excellent illustration.

She is not happy with the explanation that cross-sex discourse only reflects "the male control of macro institutions in society" (Zimmerman & West 1975: 125). Power in language, she believes, is not a measure of dominance, control, and influence but a measure of "the ability to effectively communicate and to accomplish successful discourse" (Valentine 1986: 75). She sees power as "effective comunication, an accomplishment understood to be satisfying in itself" (1985: 196) and as "a strategy that affirms the patterns found in females' and males' speech" (1986: 75). Accordingly, she proceeds to examine the strategies of "discourse topic initiation and the success rate in gaining an appropriate response and in establishing a common theme, how this discourse topic is maintained or shifted, and the organizational devices used to regulate verbal contact and conversation" (1986: 75). The discourses examined come mostly from Hindi and Indo-Anglian novels and plays.

The most important empirical findings of Valentine (1986) are: (a) "the male speaker initiates conversational topics more often than the female speaker of either Hindi or Indian English" (77); (b) whereas the male speaker's questions generally (62 percent) demand a response, the female speaker's questions are almost always (78 percent) used as a conversation maintenance device (77-78); (c) the female speaker's "utterances do not demand a response nor ensure the success of her topic and turn" (78); (d) the male speaker "rarely" makes verbal acknowledgements in response to his partner's remarks and shifts topics abruptly (80); and (e) a comparison of Hindi and Indian English cross-sex conversations intimates that the underlying sociolinguistic conventions are being transferred from the first language and first culture to English (85).

The finer empirical details of her findings can be gathered from Table 1.

	Indian English		Hindi	
	Female	Male	Female	Male
TOPICS RAISED	60	87	54	64
% raised	60/147 (41%)	87/147 (59%)	54/118 (46%)	64/118 (54%)
% with question	17/60 (28%)	36/87 (41%)	26/54 (48%)	23/64 (36%)
% with statement	43/60 (72%)	51/87 (59%)	28/54 (52%)	41/64 (64%)
Successful				
% with question	11/17 (65%)	29/36 (81%)	17/26 (65%)	29/23 (87%)
% with statement	25/43 (58%)	39/51 (76%)	15/28 (54%)	33/41 (87%)
Total	36/60 (60%)	68/87 (78%)	32/54 (59%)	53/64 (83%)

Source: Valentine (1986: 77)

TABLE 1.
Analysis of female-male topic initiation
and appropriate response success rate

Valentine suggests that the first four findings are to be "understood in terms of contributions to the conversation for better comunication" (80). "For the female speaker the power of effective communication lies in her strategies of tying together and linking utterances to establish support and create continuity in conversation" (79). For the male speaker, on the other hand, the power lies in having "his discourse topic acknowledged, secured, adopted and developed" (79). According to Valentine, there is no question of male speakers claiming "conversational control over female speakers" here. What is involved is, quite simply, "the mutual attainment of effective communication" (79) through the use of different strategies or differential use of the same strategy (as in the case of the question form).

The last finding, she argues, is to be understood within the framework of the transfer of rhetoric hypothesis. "The formal features and verbal skills particular to male and female speakers of an Indian language, such as Hindi, are transferred to the Indian variety of English by Indian users and authors" (26).

As far as the last finding is concerned, the fact that Hindi and Indian English yield "similar numbers and results" shows nothing at all, for Valentine provides no numbers and results for "English." Moreover, the facts that are available elsewhere would seem to suggest that even for English we have "similar numbers and results" (cf. Maltz & Borker 1982; West & Zimmerman 1983; Zimmerman & West 1975; and, lest we should forget, Lakoff 1973).

But suppose that there are some relevant facts of English that are different from those of Hindi and Indian English. Does that automatically entitle one to claim what Valentine claims? Structural parallelism, even in bilingual settings, does not guarantee interference. Contact induced interference must be shown to exist, not merely presupposed and asserted. The existence of similarities noted by her do not amount to much.

Consider, for example, Afrikaans and Irish English (discussed in Lass 1986). It is all too easy to say, as Hickey (1983) does, that the "pertinence" interpretation of sentences like *The soup boiled over on me* is derived from Irish *orm* because it is as common in American English as it is in Irish English. The claim that "the over-representation of the definite article" in sentences like *He likes the life abroad* can be traced back to Irish definite article before abstracts (e.g., *an fhealsunacht*) is equally untenable. The definite article is used to reify the act of living and the sentence containing it, as Lass correctly points out, is not synonymous with *He likes living abroad.*

Similarly, the violation of "verb-last in subordinate clause" rule of Afrikaans in sentences like *He hat gese, hy was siek* can be attributed to English influence only if one ignores the fact that this violation also occurs under identical syntactic conditions in German and Frisian. It is the absence of the complementizer *dat* that is responsible for the violation and not the influence of English (for further details, see Lass 1986: 86ff).

Valentine's interpretation of her findings (a-d) could profitably be dubbed "the power of the door-mat hypothesis" (cf. Chick 1985). The Valentinian power of the Indian female speaker lies in her meeting the expectations the Indian male speaker has of her. The situation is quite comparable to the situation in South Africa where Zulu-English speakers are expected to use what Chick calls "powerless language" or risk being labeled unreliable and arrogant. The success Valentine so often invokes is the success of what may be appropriately called nonparticipatory or pseudo-participatory discourse, the sort of successful discourse one can have with one's doormat.

To describe the insult of unwarrantedly shifting the topic of conversation as merely "abrupt topic shift" and the impeachment of the illocutionary force of the question as merely its transformation into "a conversational maintenance device" is only slightly more subtle than relabeling the plight of the victim of domination as "strategic maintenance of conversation." It is not clear precisely what Valentine expects from a situation in which power, the existence of which she does acknowledge (75), did play some role. How would discourse be different in the context of what she calls "hierarchical social structures" (75)?

The situation of communication harmony requires what McCarthy (1978: 325) calls an "effective equality of chances to assume dialogue roles." Valentine's findings underline the absence of that equality (see her findings (a) and (b) in particular). The interpretive devices required to defuse the inequality she does find boggle the mind of at least this speaker of (Indian?) English. They also cast doubt on not only uncritical extensions of contemporary American interactionist sociolinguistics but also on that way of doing sociolinguistics even back home in North America (cf. Singh, Lele, & Martohardjono 1988). It could hardly be otherwise. We hope its nonrelevance abroad will generate some reflection on its alleged relevance back home, the territory Hymes (1983) so tellingly refers to as "an under-developed country".

Notice that this double jeopardy argues for something more than a mere hands-off relativist position. The model under scrutiny fails both in India and back home, because it ignores hierarchical power. We can begin to get a glimpse of the distortions introduced by it only by undertaking a detailed analysis of the power relations that provide the social context for the discourses analyzed. Consider, for example, some of the speakers whose discourses Valentine analyzes. They are Westernized Indians living, temporarily, in the United States. This calls attention to at least the following two facts: (a) these speakers are elites within their own society; and (b) as far as the center is concerned, they are elites from the periphery. It is the unraveling of the parameters of power that will show what is not, but could and, therefore, ought to be, the case.

Either we could indulge in name calling or we could try and resolve the problem empirically. One way to resolve the problem empirically would be to look at at least four other kinds of discourses. In order for Valentine to make the claim that she makes and for me (S) to make the claims that I have sustained, what one would have to do is to look at four other kinds of discourses. Those would be female-female discourses with a comparable power differential. Fortunately in the 20th century the number of women managers is large enough to provide situations of that kind, where one female is in a superior position and the other female in a subordinate position. One would also have to look at male-male discourses with a comparable power differential one, and also at male-female discourses in matriarchical societies, if there are any left.

The fourth type of discourse one will have to look at is male-female discourses in context in which male speakers are in a subordinate position.

The point is one could indulge in name-calling or one can resolve the question empirically, but in order to resolve the problem, one would at least have to look at four other kinds of discourses. The conclusion is that I agree with Valentine that we must tune our instrument, language, in this case, but in order to tune this instrument we must know what we must tune it to. Her hypothesis is that we need to tune it to a kind of discourse-success as seen from the point of view of those who participate in the discourse. My hypothesis is that we must tune it to the dimension of power. This is the hypothesis.

The conclusion is fortunately an empirical one. Neither Valentine nor anybody else has looked into these four kinds of discourses. In order to provide a principled answer to what might be involved, that's what we have to do. If it turns out that it is in fact power which is the essential dimension involved here, then looking at these four kinds of discourses one would find exactly the same kinds of number and figures, or at least comparable numbers and figures, that she finds in the case of male female speakers that she looks at. This means that any subordinate position will give roughly the same kind of results. If my hunch is correct, Valentine is not talking about women's speech, let alone Indian women's speech, but about the speech of people perceived as less than equals. What is at issue is not man vs woman, but equality, something it is the business of power to minimize in practice and maximize in rhetoric.

9. ON "NON-NATIVE" ENGLISHES

> *English is not a space. It is a piece of real estate. Its owners — whose biological identities keep changing, of course, as in the case of any real estate — enforce normative spelling, punctuation, grammar, and phonological and lexical limits (within which accents and dictions may vary) throughout the domains of English discourse.*
>
> P. Dasgupta 1993: 203

According to some, contemporary sociolinguistics deserves special credit for discovering what some call "New Englishes" and for establishing a whole new "field of study." In this lecture, I'd like to look at what that is all about. What I want to talk about today, in other words, is: How things like Singapore English (SE) and Indian English (IE) have been looked at, talked about, or described, and whether there is any warrant in talking about them in this way.

The reason for putting these three things, "new","non-native" and "deviant" together should be obvious. I take the change from *deviant* to *non-native* to *new* to be licenced by the same sort of linguistic conventions, whatever they are, that allow the *department of war* to be later called the *department of defense*, or *foreign students* to be later referred to as *overseas students*, or *underdeveloped countries* to be later referred to as *developing countries*, or in Rhode Island U.S.A., *Victory over Japan Day* to be later renamed as *Veterans' Day*. Whatever is involved in this sort of terminological change is what licences my equating of "new", "non-native", and "deviant".

Taking my clue from German Romanticism, I shall begin with "non-native". The notion of NATIVE SPEAKER, as we understand it in contemporary linguistics, ultimately has its genesis in German Romanticism, where a call was issued by the Romantics that in order to describe and understand the nature and structure of language, it was not sufficient merely to describe the standardized speech of elite speakers from the centre. It was, they argued, necessary for the philologist to go out and look at the speech of ordinary people and describe that speech with the same fidelity, with the same commitment, with which the speech of the elite speakers was described at that time. The reason for appealing to German Romanticism arises because of the paradox formulated in (1) below:

(1) Although IE and SE are varieties of English, IE and SE speakers are not native speakers of English.

Standard statements about varieties or dialects of English such as Indian English and Singapore English lead straightforwardly to the paradox above. These amount to saying essentially that although Indian English and Singapore English are varieties of English, speakers of Indian English and Singapore English are NOT native speakers of English. That is the general, hopefully not uncharitable, summary of what most of the talk about Indian English and Singapore English amounts to.

Contrast these statements with the definition of native-speaker I provide in (2). I apologise for taking the liberty of citing myself:

(2) A native speaker of a language is a person who has relatively stable and consistent grammaticality judgements, which s/he shares with some other speakers, regarding structures and expressions alleged to be from his/her language (Singh 1994: 232).

If one contrasts standard statements about Indian or Singapore English with what is given in (2), the definition of Native speaker which derives ultimately from German Romanticism, what emerges is interesting. But, first the definition: it says that a native speaker of a language is a person who has a relatively stable and consistent grammaticality judgement which he or she shares with other speakers regarding structures and expressions alleged to be from his language. Any structural description of language assumes that the native speaker of a language is a person who has these judgements and who is relatively consistent in holding them — that's what makes a speaker a native speaker of whatever he is supposed to be a native speaker of. Given a definition of this sort, it is perhaps worthwhile to look at the sort of things one can say and compare them with the sort of things that have been said. Consider the statements in (3) below:

(3) (a) Speakers of Canadian English are not native speakers of British, Irish, Indian, or Singapore English.

(b) Native speakers of Singapore English are not native speakers of American, Indian, or Irish English.

One could make statements of the type I have given in (3a and b). These are reasonable but trivial statements, meaning they are true but trivially so. One is entitled to say, in my view, that speakers of Canadian English are not native speakers of British, Indian or Singaporean English. This is a true statement in my view, but, I repeat, an entirely trivial one. One can also say that native speakers of Singaporean English are not native speakers of American, Indian, or Irish English.

Now contrast these statements with what appears in (4) below:

(4) (a) Speakers of Appalachian English are not native speakers of English.

(b) Speakers of Singapore English are not native speakers of English.

These statements are, perhaps a bit uncharitably, best characterized as incomprehensible statements. Perhaps the modifier *incomprehensible* is simply an admission of personal defeat. I don't understand what these sentences could possibly mean. One can say, as has sometimes been said, that speakers of Applachian English are not native speakers of American English, or speakers of Singaporean English are not native speakers of British English. But, I confess that I cannot understand, cannot interpret, the statements in (4). The reason that it seems difficult to understand sentences like (4 a and b) is that I am unable to decipher what the content of the predicate "not-native" might be.

The other reason is, essentially, that those who describe these varieties seem to be constructing mini-museums. They take isolated pieces, exotic items, from these languages, put them together, and des-cribe their collections. That is what I refer to as museum construction. There are various ways of constructing these mini-museums. Some of them are exemplified in (5) below:

(5) Museology

(a) German has the following rule of word-final devoicing:

$$\begin{bmatrix}\text{obs}\\ \text{+voice}\end{bmatrix} \text{-->} [\text{-voice}] \; / \; \_\_ \; \#$$

(b) English has the following rule of vowel lengthening:

$$[\text{V}] \text{-->} [\text{+long}] \; / \; \_\_ \begin{bmatrix}\text{C}\\ \text{+voice}\end{bmatrix}$$

So, one can indulge in descriptive exercises like (5a and b). One can say that German has a rule of word final devoicing or that English has a rule of vowel lengthening, i.e., vowels are normally lengthened in English (at least in some varieties of English) when they are followed by a voiced consonant.

One can do a bit more. One could construct somewhat more complicated museums than the ones illustrated in (5), the sort illustrated in (6) below:

(6) Simple Comparative Exercises:

	German	English	Dutch	Sanskrit
Word-final Devoicing	+	-	+	+
Epenthesis	+	+	+	+

One could, in other words, construct descriptive statements of the sort that appear in (6), by setting up processes and languages in columns and rows. One could say, for example, that there is a process or a rule, whatever terminology you prefer, called WORD-FINAL DEVOICING, and that it is found in German but not in English. One can look at another rule, let us say, epenthesis, which introduces a vowel that appears under certain circumstances and discover that German, English, Dutch, and Sanskrit all have it. Now, these are all harmless, innocent bits of museum-construction.

But there is another type of museum that one could construct. Some examples appear under (7). These comparative exercises I have labelled as pathological, again perhaps a bit uncharitably:

(7) Some Pathological Comparative/Contrastive Exercises:

(a) Unlike Standard British English (SBE), Cameroonian English uses an invariant tag (Todd 1986)

(b) Canadians, unlike Americans, raise the nucleus of a diphthong when it is followed by a voiceless consonant (Joos 1942)

(c) Whereas British speakers pronounce the voiceless alveolar stop robustly in all contexts, Americans flap it in the intervocalic position.

(d) IE speakers often substitute [t̪] or [t^h] for English [θ] (Hansen-Bhatt 1992).

Let us take (7b). One could say that Canadian English, unlike American English, raises the nucleus where the diphthong is followed by a voiceless consonant, so that Americans say [wɑɪf] and Canadians say [wʌɪf]. The onglide is slightly higher and the vowel has a slightly different quality. Or take (7c). One could say that British speakers pronounce the voiceless alveolar stop /t/ in contexts in which Americans flap it. What some Britishers refer to as [torɔnto] is by some speakers of American English pronounced as [torõᴅo]. One could say, as in fact has been said, that Indian English speakers often substitute a dental /t/ or aspirate /t/ for English /θ/.

Some rather naive questions come to mind when one looks at these complicated museums. Why should the Cameroonian, or Irish, or Indian care what the British or the American does or does not do. Perhaps more importantly, the question is what could he do , even if he did care?

What one could do is construct upside down museums as a possible response to what seems to be a somewhat less than rational exercise. This is exemplified in (8):

(8) Reverse Museology:

(a) Unlike IE, BE uses several question tags.

(b) Americans, unlike Canadians, show lack of phonetic sophistication in not making a distinction between *rider* and *writer*.

(c) Whereas Americans use the natural process of flapping the intervocalic /t/, British speakers suppress that natural process.

(d) AE, BE, and CE speakers substitute [θ] for IE [t̪].

Let us take (8a): one could say that, unlike Indian English, British English uses several tags. Or, take (8b): one could say that Americans, unlike Canadians, show lack of phonetic sophistication in not making a distinction between *writer* and *rider*, which Canadians do and Americans don't. One could, as suggested in (8c), also say that whereas Americans use the natural process of flapping the inter-vocalic /t/, the British speakers suppress that entirely natural process. Or one could go all the way and say that American, British and Canadian English substitute /θ/ for Indian English dental /t̪/. The point of this exercise is to highlight the synchronic absurdity of statements of this type, with the plea that the absurdity here is qualitatively not very different from the absurdity assumed or implied under (7).

Some of the difficulties associated with (7) and (8) are sketched out in (9):

(9) Difficulties with (7)

(a) Even if true, statements such as 7a-b are largly irrelevant.

(b) Generally, they are not true, and that, in both directions.

(i) CE, for example, DOES use other tag-types.

(ii) AE/BE/CE DO in fact use the invariant tag.

(c) Vitiation by unwarranted intrusion of variability (It is unjustifiably assumed that all varieties have the same underlying form)

(d) English = Standard British/American English

Even if true, statements such as those in (7) are largely irrelevant. What do I mean by largely irrelevant? Let us take (7b). There is no reason to consider what Americans do or what Americans don't do. The data is not available to the speaker of Canadian English who is trying to construct his or her grammar to cope with such facts.

Unfortunately, these statements are not only irrelevant for the construction of synchronic grammars of the variety that one is looking at, generally they are not even true. And they are not true bi-directionally, so that, for example, Cameroonian English does in fact use other tag types. It is not true that it only uses invariant tags. The other side is also false: it is not correct to say that American, Canadian, or British English do not use the invariant tag, for they actually do: American English uses *O.K.* and Canadian English uses *eh*. Even if one were charitable and were to consider statements like these as somewhat relevant for some purposes, they happen empirically not to be true.

The other difficulty associated with them is that they are vitiated by an unwarranted intrusion of variability. What I mean by that is that when one is constructing the grammar of a particular variety, the sources of data available to the speaker are restricted in ways these statements don't acknowledge. The form that the grammar of a person is likely to have can't be based on data not available to that speaker. If one is not exposed to something, if the language input of the speaker does not include the data from another variety, from another dialect, then it seems hard to understand how that evidence could be taken into account in the construction of that speaker's grammar. Perhaps a word of clarification is in order: when I say GRAMMAR. I am not talking about books that are normally referred to as grammars, I am talking about the grammar that the speakers of language can be legitimately said to have in order to use the language that they in fact use.

Another difficulty with the statements of the sort that appear under (7) is that, generally, discussions of varieties of English make the assumption that English means Standard British English or Standard American English. So that when one talks about Indian English or Singaporean English, one contrasts what goes on in Indian English and Singaporean English with what goes on in Standard English, American and/or British English. One normally does not talk about what happens in Alabama, Texas, Liverpool, or Dublin. These details are carefully kept outside the discussion.

Precisely because details of this kind are kept outside the discussion, one is entitled to ask a couple of very naive questions (formulated in 10 below):

(10) What is an "NN" variety?

- (a) Do they have any uniquely non-English (= not attested/possible in any variety labelled "native") properties (lexical, morphological, phonological, syntactic, functional, registral etc)?
- (b) If they are defined, each one of them, as a unique cluster of non-unique properties or features, they are just like so-called "native" varieties, aren't they?

What is in fact a "new"/"non-native" variety? One possible way to answer that question is to say that perhaps a "new"/"non-native" variety is a variety of English which has some uniquely non-English features, where English stands for what is referred to as "native" English, and these features are neither attested nor possible in any of the varieties otherwise called "native".

These features and properties, if the traditional enterprise of linguistics has any validity, can be only half a dozen types, namely lexical, morphological, phonological, syntactical, functional and registral. One could argue that the search for unique features that characterize these so called "new"/"non-native" varieties is partially misguided, and that what one ought to do is not look for one unique property of these things but clusters of properties that make these varieties unique. But if one were to take that position, one would find oneself in great difficulty, since all dialects and all varieties are in fact unique clusters of non-unique properties. If one were to take the approach outlined in (10b), all that one can do is establish that a variety or type is or is not a variety or type. It will have no bearing on the question whether it should be classified as "new"/"non-native". Therefore, it becomes imperative to raise the question of what I call "the limits of native variability."

Let us assume for a minute that there is some content in the word *native*, or the word *old*, or the word *normal*. The question to ask is what are the limits of variability permitted within the so-called "native" dialects or "native" varieties. They could be either functional or domain-related: these varieties may differ from each other in terms of their functions and domain strength.

But if one looks at the literature about Indian English and Singapore English, one repeatedly finds claims of the sort that appear in (11):

(11) (a) "the penetration of English into several domains" (Pakir 1991: 167).

(b) "domain separation is beginning to disappear" (Sahgal 1991: 105).

It has become quite clear that domain penetration is fairly substantial and that on grounds of domain differentiation or functional needs, Indian and Singaporean English cannot in fact be considered as anything different from what would otherwise be described as "native", or "old", or whatever adjective you prefer. It is possible to look for differences in register. Again, to the best of my knowledge, no evidence has been provided that there are any registral difference in these varieties. One could look at morphology to see if there are any differences in morphological structures of Singapore English or Indian English, as opposed to British or Canadian English or whatever varieties or dialects one wishes to look at. In this context, it is rather surprising that one does not find a single word in the literature, unless my reading has been excessively limited, which is not allowed by the rules of some other so-called native variety of English. It is quite possible to find words in Singapore English or Indian English that do not exist in British English or American English. That, again, is a true but irrelevant observation. What is relevant is: are there words in these varieties that are not sanctioned or not allowed or that cannot be constituted on the basis of what is possible within any so-called "native" variety?

In the literature, again, there is discussion about "deviation" of the sort that appears in the syntax of Indian English and Singapore English. Here it is sufficient to recall that that kind of statement becomes possible if and only if one is concentrating exclusively on Standard American or Standard British. One does not have to go very far to find syntactic structures or sentences of the type that otherwise appear to be "non-native":

(12) (a) might could, might better, used to could (Scotland and Florida)

(b) I want for him to go (Ottawa Valley, Canada)

(c) He's gone a-fishing (Oregon, U.S.A. and Newfoundland, Canada)

The list could be multiplied *ad infinitum*, but there is no need to do so. Identically, if one looks at phonological matters, one sometimes finds statements of the kind that there is something peculiar in what is done in Singapore English or what is done in Indian English. That sort of statement of peculiarity rests exclusively on the fact that "marginal", "non-standard" varieties of English in contexts otherwise known as "native" have not been looked at. It is actually quite common to find retroflection in Scottish English and dentalization in Irish English. It is also quite common to find non-reduction of vowels in American English. And the differences between the stress and accent placement between British and American English have been well known enough to have been incorporated even into some text books.

Perhaps the last place that one can look for these differences is in the lexicon, but here again it is difficult to see why differences in the lexicon could define in any way the variations in these dialects as unique, or as somehow different. Under (13), I list some of the words taken from McArthur (1986; cited in D'Souza 1992):

(13) Lexical

(i) IE *goonda* 'a scoundrel'; AE *zilch* 'nothing at all'

SE *burn* 'a stream'; HE *mahalo* 'thank you'.

That these words have roughly the same status should be obvious. There is, in other words, no reason to believe that there is something funny about the Hawaiian word for 'Thank you' any more than there might be about the Scottish word for stream. So one must answer, minimally, the question of what the limits of native variability are, before one can use terms such as "native" or "non-native" in order to classify the dialects and varieties of English the way they have been classified.

Now we have a good idea of the dimensions along which one can look for these differences, but, in the final analysis, a lot of attestations would have to be checked and a lot of dialect atlases would have to be consulted. This enterprise is limited, and, in the final analysis, really not relevant. It is not relevant because attestation has obvious limitations. What one has to look at is the possibility allowed by these so called "native" dialects. The sort of question that arises here is: what could one say if it were to turn out that some feature of some of these varieties is rather unique? Here one has to ask the question of the sort that can be illustrated with the history of, say, Punjabi. At some point it acquired tone (in the sense that it became a lexical property and it has some morphological function). Does one say that the moment it acquired tone, it was no longer Punjabi? Or, that Punjabi is no longer an Indic language. I am assuming that there is general agreement that that is too drastic a statement to make, i.e., it really is not possible to say that Punjabi is no longer an Indic language. In other words, if we look again in the realm of possibilities, then it may turn out that attestation, though revealing and certainly enlightening in various ways, at times turns out to have its own limitations. I conclude that the only criterion for deciding whether a speaker is or is not a native speaker is as formulated in (2) above, which, at the risk of being repetitious, I'll share with you again:

(14) A native speaker of a language is a person who has relatively stable and consistent grammaticality judgements, which s/he shares with some other speakers, regarding structures and expressions alleged to be from his/her language (Singh 1994: 232).

It says that a native speaker of a language is a person who has relatively stable and consistent grammaticality judgement which she/he shares with some speakers regarding structures and expressions alleged to be from her/his language. That's the only criterion we seem to be left with.

One could perhaps argue that this might work to a certain extent, but that there are perhaps differences in the history and origin of these languages. Let's play with another set of labels that have been used in second language acquisition literature and say that there are such things as English, German, and Dutch, and they are to be called primary languages and there are things to be called non-primary languages, and that these are the things that a learner is said to be learning. Indian and Singapore English are, thus, non-primary languages. But even if historically Singapore, Indian and Camaroonian English can be shown to be the res-ults of contact induced inter-languages, synchronically they are not non-primary. Besides, criteria for distinguishing between primary and non-primary languages are very hard to find, and actually I don't know of any.

One could bring other kinds of objections. A "new"/"non-native" variety is, one could argue, not learnt as a first language. My response to that would be quite simple — So what? Unilingualism can't be a defining property of "nativeness". Once internal sharing has been established within a community, then anyone who participates in that community by definition is a native speaker, irrespective of that person being mono-, bi- or multilingual.

One could suggest yet other criteria. One could say that a non-variety becomes a variety when it meets or is accorded institutional approval. That raises the sort of question that is best formulated as: "Did Yale have no American-speaking faculty members until Yale senate officially voted or allowed lectures in American English?" That happened in 1929 and before that it was illegal to lecture at Yale in American English. So much for institutional approval. Some scholars, such as Quirk (1991), have also invoked the notion of state approval. That, in my mind, raises the question: "Was the author of *Dhammapada* not a native speaker of Pali, despite the fact that it was not recognized by the state, including his own?" Another kind of criterion that one can suggest is that these varieties have a special, funny status because they have not been standardized, because these varieties have emerging but unrecognized status. Again, my first naive question is: "recognized by who?" My second, not so naive question is: "Were there no native speakers of Sanskrit before Panini?" Wasn't Panini actually one of the last native speakers of Sanskrit? Sanskrit was not standardized before he wrote the grammar, presumably 5th century B.C. It would, however, be unreasonable to conclude from that that he was not a native speaker of Sanskrit. One can also ask ques-tions like: "Are there in fact no native speakers of Eskimo or Montagnais, two of the Canadian languages that have no full reference grammars?"

Perhaps there is a larger question related to the issue of having standardized reference grammars. Do ethnographically uncharted communities in fact not exist? What about communities that do not sanction non-participatory observer roles? We all know that there are social communities in this world for which an ethnographic description has not been provided, for which social grammars have not been constructed. I think it will be less than reasonable to deny them the status of communities. Perhaps one could ask the next question: Do we in fact have a grammar of any community or culture? The fact that we don't, should not, I submit, allow us to say that those communities and cultures in fact do not exist. Or, to take a concrete example, one can ask "Does Breton in France not exist because the French Academy does not concern itself with it?", "Does the sharing among Breton speakers in France have no standing, no status?" It will be unreasonable to say that these are not native speakers of this language and that this community does not exist.

Another kind of objection or another kind of criterion has been suggested for these "new"/"non-native" varieties. They have, we are told, more variability. I'd like to argue that it merely seems that way. The acquisition of a language by speakers is generally confused in these contexts with the acquisition of speakers by a language, so that when one describes a situation like that of India or Singapore, one is generally not keeping these two categories apart. I am talking about those who have learned the language, not about those who have been only recently acquired by the language that the former group has in fact learned. The other factor that enters in this picture is that the "other" always appears monolithic. Quite frankly, I am puzzled by the fact that socio-linguists can say this sort of thing and pay homage to Labov at the same time. His work has repeatedly documented the kind of variability that is involved in so-called "native" contexts. So what is variable in these contexts is not so much language as its demographic status. The variability of American English, for example, is not a function of the percentage of speakers using it in the U.S.A.

Ironically, study after study of these so called "non-native" contexts shows that the variability that does exist in these places has its own structure, again quite consistent with the sort of predictions that Labov will make. The conclusion to draw from these studies is not to say that there is more variability in these places but that another kind of variability is also involved. Another kind of argument that is sometimes used in the literature to make the case that there is something funny about Indian and Singapore English is that there is no agreement about these things: one does not really know how to define Singapore or Indian English. Notice that this objection or criterion raises serious problems if one reflects on the status of, for example, General American back in North America. It will be perhaps sufficient to recall that there are fairly respectable linguists in the U.S.A. that describe what is called General American as "North East Fantasy". The point here is that these so-called "native" grounds provide reasons to believe that the projection of Standard British or American English is not as monolithically supported as those who support them outside would like us to believe. R.P., for example is the speech of no more than 4% of British speakers. A book like Jacob Mey's (1985) *Whose Language* raises precisely the question that is raised in the context of "new"/"non-native" varieties. Mey asks the question: Whose language? and in fact points out that even on home ground, these questions are not as simple as they appear to be. Constructs such as British English, American English, are fraught exactly with the same problems as constructs such as Indian and Singapore English might be.

Another objection is that there is something funny about these varieties because they often have speakers that use external models. My response to that kind of criterion can be summarized in the form of a question: "Does Henry James learning to speak like an Englishman cease to be a native speaker of English?" My question is what happens to him at that point. Does he cease to be a native speaker of English, merely because he was trying to change his variety?

The last argument invoked in the literature about making a distinction about these groups or varieties that I am familiar with is what is referred to as the mutual intelligibility criterion. The argument has been made that if the monolithic constructs called Standard British or American English are to be retained, then mutual intelligibility is guaranteed. There are serious problems with mutual intelligibility. To the best of my knowledge, the phonological system of Quebec French has not undergone any change since the sixties, but, interestingly, the intelligibility of Quebec French can be said to have increased. There was a time when it was necessary for a speaker of Parisian French not to understand Quebec French. Actually, such a speaker would be rather caught dead than admit that he understood Quebec French. Now things seem to be different. Perhaps the reason for this is located outside of linguistics. At any rate, the phonological system of Quebec has not undergone any change, but mutual intelligibilty has increased considerably.

Then there is the famous problem of Icelandic and Faroese. It is a classic case in which speakers of Faroese have no difficulty understanding Icelandic and speakers of Icelandic are rather proud of the fact that they do not understand Faroese. The systems are almost identical. Then there is the question of intelligibility of Standard British English. Whereas Standard British English is indeed very intelligible to elite upper class speakers even in the United States, particularly to Boston

Brahmins, non-elite speakers of American English find it rather unintelligible. There are, then, serious difficulties with notion of mutual intelligibility, and I take it that whatever is involved has to do with language only in a marginal way.

The tasks we have before us, I believe, are best summarized as follows:

(15) (a) Just as a native speaker is able to make sense of his being a native speaker with other native speakers, the scholar must make sense of their native speakers' language not FOR them but WITH them.

(b) Our second task must, therefore, be that if labels such as "new" and "non-native" are in fact devoid of any content, the scholar must expose the reasons for which the differences and exotica have been emphasized and these labels have been used.

I believe some rather interesting ironies become apparent after some reflection on "new"/"non-native" Englishes. Some of them are listed in (16) below:

(16) (a) It is perhaps no accident that it was Queen Isabella's sociolinguists who took away the pride the young Spanish boy outside Madrid had in his vernacular. I remind you that it was at the time of Queen Isabella that teaching of Standard Spanish was implemented as the official policy on the recommendations of sociolinguists of that time.

(b) The second irony or moral seems to be that those who want to set up standards for Indian and Singapore English may find themselves in a bind because others are a bit eager to set up standards for THEM.

(c) The third irony is that the participants in the discussion on "new"/"non-native" varieties,

> particularly the South Asian or South East Asian participants, seem to be asking for some kind of special status for these varieties, forgetting that to ask for a special status is to ask for it on the terms of the giver.

And perhaps the biggest irony of all is that, as Dasgupta (1993) argues, these varieties may not be SOCIALLY justified because the requirement of community that MY discussion takes to have been met may actually be said to not have been met in places like India and Singapore. That would be the biggest irony because those who claim to have won a place of pride for varieties such as IE and SE claim to have done so from what they like to refer to as "the socio-linguistic perspective." The issue of the communitization of speakers of IE and SE is a very complex one, and all I can do here is to refer you, once again, to Dasgupta's illuminating refusal to grant the status of a community to users of English in places like India, and to add that our sociolinguists appear to have done well only because they have, perhaps predictably, looked both at the structural and the social only superficially.

It is worth quoting Dasgupta (personal communication) on the issue of communitization :

> "The single most important issue, to my mind, is whether an IE community of some sort exists on non-Kachruvian grounds. This is a contested question, to a greater degree than is usual with social facts (which are of course all contestable); the ease with which NRI [non-resident Indians] has taken over the quintessential IE writer seems to indicate that NRIs and RNIs [resident non-Indians] together, lumpenly, lead SOME straggling body of Indian followers; English medium schooling may create a larger constituency for those of them who would like to claim community status for this leadership and its followership; but most of the NRI/RNI leadership seems to feel that it will be bad business to ghettoize themselves into an IE community, better business to buy into an ethnically tinged mainstream Anglophony; hence the stragglingness of their followers in India who polish-their-accent-but-not-beyond-a-certain-point, and who are unsure as to what they are polishing towards. I think the empirical base for figuring out what is happening to the option of the communitization of IE is in Anglophonia and would call for (at least) phonological investigation. Not knowing how such an inquiry would turn out, I am really neutral

> on whether there is, or is going to be, or is going to remain, a sustained identity of IE speakership, coupled with its those-who-made-it creamy layer actually residing in metro-Anglophonia. My book [cf. Dasgupta 1993] merely makes a statement about how people living in India use English and what this mode of use seems to mean in India. This statement is necessarily incomplete, and may, as it stands, mislead readers at certain points. I do hope future work will be more sensitive to the current of positive claims for an IE community"

Given that neither "native"/"non-native" nor "new/old" is sustainable — some "old" varieties are newer than some "new" varieties — perhaps IE, SE etc. can be grouped together, if they must be grouped together, under the label "Doubly Disowned" i.e., disowned both by their native-speakers and by native-speakers of other varieties. But even that label may have to include Australian English (and perhaps even most dialects of Arabic). It does, however, have the advantage of not having any diachronic or synchronic connotations.

10. THE DICTIONARY AS AN INTRODUCTION TO SOCIOLINGUISTICS

And so each venture
Is a new beginning, a raid against the inarticulate

T.S. Eliot 1942

Ever since Cawdrey (1604), one of the "official" aims of lexicography has been to gather interpretations for "the benefit and helpe" of "unskillfull persons". With the banishment of the sort of humour Cockeram (1623), who defined "phylologie" as "love of much babbling", could display, the English dictionary becomes the official warehouse of the ideological prejudices of the dominant elites, all under the name of what Kersey (1702) calls "clear exposition", for the benefit of what Bullokar (1616) refers to as "the capacity of the ignorant".

In this lecture, I'd like (1) to trace the "standardization" of the lexicographical discourse of definitions up to the point where the dictionary becomes a tool in the manufacture of consent that requires the devaluation of all currencies except the scientistic, (2) to illustrate how ruler-oriented opacity is enshrined in dictionaries, and (3) to offer a few illustrations of non-opaque definitions that might actually be of some benefit to "unskillful persons". Inasmuch as the dictionary is an unparallelled source for an understanding of the generalized version of what Chomsky (1985) calls "Orwell's Problem", the problem which has been the focus of Critical Theory (cf. Habermas 1979), it is an extremely valuable introduction to sociolinguistics.

We tend to take our dictionary for granted: an awareness of its force may be aroused if we study the slow growth and gradual accretions through which it has evolved.

The first English dictionary, *A Table Alphabeticall*, was written by Robert Cawdrey in 1604. It was, of course, preceded by several bilingual dictionaries, among which the Latin-English lexicons were particularly important and influential. The growing vocabulary of the English language during the Renaissance, and more particularly the import into English of words from foreign and especially classical languages, created a large body of new vocabulary of the sciences and geographical explorations. The spirit of Renaissance nationalism and a growing interest in the vernacular gave an impetus to the creation of the English dictionary combined with the pedagogical method of the interlinear gloss to provide its format. Cawdrey's *A Table Alphabeticall* carries on its title page the following inscription:

> "A Table Alphabeticall, conteyning and teaching the true writing, and understanding of hard usuall English words, borrowed from the Hebrew, Greeke, Latine, or French, &c. With the interpretation thereof by plaine English words, gathered for the benefit & helpe of Ladies, Gentlewomen, or any other unskilfull persons."

The English dictionary's emphasis on hard words from the beginning and its professed aim to assist the less privileged towards a better understanding of their own language, may appear reassuring to those of us who have since childhood viewed the dictionary as a book in which one looks up the meanings and spellings of difficult words. But the dictionary, though it may still seem to fulfill these elementary requirements, has "advanced" beyond them to embody the intellectual history of the whole civilization of the people using it.

After Cawdrey had taken the major step of compiling an alphabetical list of words and providing definitions, even though meagre and simple, the "hard-word" character of the English dictionary was temporarily established. John Bullokar, for instance, in *An English Expositor* (1616) continues to emphasize "the great store of strange words, our speech doth borrow, not only from the Latine and Greeke, (and from the ancient Hebrew) but also from forraine vulgar languages round about us ...". In Bullokar, however, the territory of hard words is extended to "sundry olde words now growne out of use, and divers terms of art, proper to the learned in Logicke, Philosophy, Law, Physicke, Astronomie, etc.", which the writer meant to open to "the capacitie of the ignorant". That is why Bullokar leaps from Cawdrey's 2500 words to almost twice as many entries.

I want to turn to its professed aim of assisting the less privileged understand the "meanings" of "difficult" words.

Chomsky (1985) correctly identifies the two major problems of epistemology as Plato's problem and Orwell's problem. Attempts to deal with the former must come to terms with the now familiar poverty of stimulus argument and those dealing with the latter with the nature and structure of "propaganda-machines" that control, manage, and distort information in order to create, foster, and sustain ideologies that impinge on mental freedom and constrain and delimit interpretation (cf. Habermas 1979). Language, as Chomsky's own work amply shows, provides a unique window for an investigation of both of these problems.

As the essence of Orwell's problem resides in the instrumental use of "idea words", what is needed is a lexicographical supplement to Chomsky's illuminating analyses of the linguistically opaque strategies used in what he calls "the manufacture of consent". This lecture will, therefore, make a modest proposal regarding what a non-opaque dictionary of the English language should look like, and present some sample entries for such a dictionary.

Standard dictionaries of English, such as the *Oxford English Dictionary* (*OED*), *Webster's Third* (*WT*), and *Hornby's Advanced Learner's Dictionary* (*ALD*), not only don't meet the challenge, which was, as I said, their original declared aim, but also serve the purpose of propagating ruler-oriented definitions of terms and expressions. Consider, for example, standard definitions of *democracy* and *politics*:

(1) *democracy*

1. government by the people; a social state in which all have rights — *OED*
2. rule by the ruled — *WT*
3. govt. in which all adult citizens share through their elected representatives — *ALD*

politics

1. the science and art of government	*OED*
2. the science and art of political government	*WT*
3. the science or art of government	*ALD*

Given the socio-economic reality of English-speaking pluralist democracies, it is, I submit, more appropriate to define these terms as follows:

(2) *democracy*: the system of socio-political organization in which elites compete for access to public resources according to well-defined rules of conduct.

politics: the arena in which competitive games, involving strategies and instrumental actions, are played by elites in order to privatise public resources.

The non-opaque definitions of (2) remove the sociolinguistic opacity embedded in those of (1) and demystify terms with which hegemonic pluralist elites legitimize their power and domination (cf. Habermas). Having argued my case with examples like *politics* and *democracy*, below I present a few more entries for a non-opaque dictionary. They include terms such as *charisma*, *entrepreneur*, *modernity* and *tradition*, and their non-opaque definitions.

aborigines: those disseminated and demographically displaced cultures and peoples victimized by the conquest and plunder of Western expansion.

activist: one who feels obliged to take courses of action in direct or indirect response to the needs and misfortunes of persons, often not unaware of the rewards that accompany the expression of critical impulses.

affluence: the condition in which a minority of the world populace maintains a level of material and caloric consumption far beyond human necessities, perhaps not unrelated to the fact that one-third of the world's population exists undernourished in abject poverty.

alienation: the removal and subsequent isolation of an individual from the affective identity and laws typical of family, kinship, tribe, or informal corporate group, and one's reintegration into productive obligations of a contractual and impersonal nature.

automation: the relinquishing of the human touch and the commonality of physical initiative, thereby giving precedence to mechanization and its domination for purposes of quantitative increase in productive output.

bargaining: a form of transaction, once reflective of varying degrees of reciprocity; now characterized by calculated exchange and the accounting of currencies and goods; standard *modus operandi* of pluralist democracies.

bribe: a contractually unspecified commission that threatens the social reputation of one party and advances that of another.

charisma: the anachronistic personal appeal of a political figure, believed to be quite common only outside Western democracies, but found to some degree in all societies, that in reality does not reflect that person's actual capacities and qualifications except for the followers that wish to believe in them.

capitalism: the present hegemonic and economic world system of surplus appropriation directed by the United States, Great Britain, France, West Germany, Japan, and Israel, its foremost enforcers.

colonialism: a system by which a dominant political structure subjugates and expropriates the human and material resources, potential wealth, and the cultural institutions of an unsuspecting and vulnerable society, often aided and supported by reward-seeking native collaborators.

commission: a contractually specified piece of the pie.

commodity: an object of use-value that is manipulated as a marketable item from which profits and capital gains are accumulated.

corruption: a semi-legal term applied to the violation of rules that govern the appropriation of public resources; used as a moral term for weaker economies victimized by the fluctuation and pressures of world marketing.

entrepreneur: one who by free-style unsanctioned economic pursuits seeks his/her own profit and therefore remains responsible to his/herself only.

feudalism: a system of well-defined rules with an unwritten provision for the distribution of private resources for public purposes.

ideology: a secular global view of human qualities, events, and intentionality that eventually exhausts itself in dogmatism.

inflation: the rise in the market value of goods and services, manipulated by hegemonic economic forces in order to protect, control, and widen multinationalism.

intellectual: one whose well-being and survival is determined by the fabrication and selling of knowledge, or someone who is a parasite on his/her own intelligence.

middle-class: the secondary interest group characteristic of industrialized societies, serving the function of rapid consumption of goods and services thereby generating wealth for elites.

peasant: one who's well-being and physical survival is based on a land-labour relationship and whose subsistence production is a prerequisite for the accumulation of surplus and wealth to others.

primitive: an ethnocentric and condescending term applied to societies considered to be lower in terms of technological, scientific, and cultural evolution when compared to the 19th and 20th century Occident.

race: such classificatory and prejudicial terms as "Caucasian", "Mongolian", "Negroid", etc. that are apparently arbitrarily imposed on the continuum of human physiognomy and anatomical traits.

> *state*: a system where legal intentionality, universal application of law, and recourse to physical coercition is invested in a body of competing elites.

It should be obvious that the critique of the dictionary as a warehouse of the sacrosanct prejudices of the dominating elites, enshrined in my deliberately exaggerated counter-definitions is related to both ordinary language philosophy and Critical theory. Some comments on these relationships are, obviously, in order.

First, ordinary language philosophy: the defenders of ordinary language as something "all right" seem to me to be quite correct in discouraging the use of technical and "logically perfect" language when ordinary language seems to do just as well, if not better. They seem to err, however, in assuming, as it were, that what is "all right" is in fact all right. Philosophical difficulties do certainly arise as a result of the philosopher misconstruing ordinary language; but not to look at why ordinary language is ordinary language is to shirk part of the philosophical responsibility. Ordinary language is indeed the correct language for describing what the jargonist describes rather tortuously and inadequately in his parlour language that rarely lasts more than a decade, and it may in fact be the correct language for ordinary speakers to use to describe what they see around them. The trouble is that the second use of the word *correct* is identical with *expected*. The ordinary speaker is expected to see the competitive game of appropriation around him as desirable and refer to it as *democracy*. It is needless to add that *expected* is essentially a transitive predicate. The defenders of ordinary language seem to take *correct* as *expected* to be the same thing as correct as accurate.

Was there perhaps a grain of truth in the logical positivist's criticism of Wittgenstein's most famous dictum? The logical positivists criticized it on the grounds that it implied that there WAS something to be silent about. They may have been right, perhaps despite themselves. Wittgenstein's silence and Buddha's *karuna* "compassion" are not enough. Sometimes, silence appears to be golden only because those who want it observed supply the gold.

Now, Critical theory. Critical theorists such as Habermas (1979,

1984 and 1987, etc.) seems particularly sensitive to the obstacles to radical change. Their work is, accordingly, largely an attempt to analyse and expose these. The focus of their work is the hiatus between the actual and the possible, and the forces that make it difficult or impossible to realize the possible contained in the actual. Each glance at the map of the world reminds them, as Wilde would have said, of the utopia that seems to have been systematically deleted, almost completely. They see it contained in the very deformed contours of the map they have been presented with, and shrouded in mystery for the ordinary eye that has been trained by forces that took it off the map. Its traces, they contend, are nevertheless there and can be brought into relief when the distortions are exposed for what they are.

The enterprise of Critical theorists of exposing the obstacles to change is necessarily conducted through language. It is, therefore, interesting to see precisely what they seem to want to do, linguistically speaking. Part of what they are trying to do is supplant ordinary language with what at the moment appears to be extra-ordinary language. Their term for it is, obviously, "development of consciousness", including, of course, "self-consciousness". There is a difference between their attempt to supplant ordinary language with their seemingly extra-ordinary language and, and this is important, some others attempting to supplant ordinary language with what might be loosely described as technical jargon. Whereas they insist on exposing the forces that have made ordinary language ordinary language, the others seem to rejoice in rejecting the ways in which ordinary speakers make sense of the world in which they live. A Critical theorist understands why ordinary speakers use the language they do — according to him, they have been put in that position and have little choice — and the jargonist places the burden squarely on the ordinary speaker. The ordinary speaker uses the language he does because he doesn't, according to the jargonist, have the technical expertise he needs to talk otherwise. It is, of course, true that the ordinary speaker doesn't talk the way the Critical theorist does, but, and that is the crux, it is not because he doesn't have the technical expertise. According to the Critical theorist, the ordinary speaker, in fact, expresses the same critique in his ordinary language as the theorist. The reason the ordinary speaker's expose or critique is not heard is that the makers or arbiters of ordinary language turn a deaf ear to the very ordinary part of ordinary language.

There is actually a sense in which what the Critical theorist does can be described as intra-lingual translation: he takes the ordinary speaker's critique (mass culture, for example) and translates it for the arbiters of not-so-ordinary part of ordinary language. The arbiters in question may not like the translation, but it is done in terms that they do UNDERSTAND (in the ordinary sense of the word *understand*). The negative predicate *don't like* translates, obviously, as *don't approve of.*

Let us take the example of *democracy* again. The essence of the Critical theorist's comments about democracy is that *democracy* should not, and therefore does not, mean what it has come to mean. It now designates merely a form of competitive behaviour consonant with the nature of capitalist economy. The Critical theorist prefers to refer to what is presented and projected as democracy as PLURALIST DEMOCRACY, just as the more sophisticated political scientists of other persuasions do. The difference seems to me to be that whereas for the former the term *pluralist* marks (in the standard linguistic sense) the term *democracy*, for the latter it merely explains it. *Democracy* and *pluralist democracy* are, in other words, interchangeable for the latter but not for the former. For the Critical theorist, the problem is to expose the ways in which pluralist democracy is projected as if it were democracy. For him, the adjectival *pluralist* is an identificational tag that contains the empirical content of the nature of democracy in the modern world. For others, pluralist democracy IS democracy; for the Critical theorist, it is a mockery of democracy. This much can be seen fairly clearly in the fact that for the Critical theorist it is the longer term that is unmarked. In some sense, whereas the Critical theorist wants people to use the word *pluralist democracy* to describe the political systems of modern industrialized societies, its apologists want them to continue using the shorter *democracy* except in highly technical discourses.

To say that what the Critical theorist wants is the replacement of the word *democracy* by the word *pluralist democracy* in ordinary language is not to say that that is all he wants. By insisting on the marked term to describe what he thinks is actually out there, he is in fact asking people, speakers of ordinary language, to see why what has become the unmarked term to describe the same reality cannot legitimately be used. The ordinary language philosopher can't see this because for him the ordinary nose is the nose that matters. He can't see how it has been systematically disinfected to such an extent that it seems now to be incapable of picking up the scent that attracts the Critical theorist.

11. CHOMSKY, LANGUAGE, AND SOCIETY

The only valid tribute to thought...is to make it groan and protest.

M. Foucault 1980: 53

I have often invoked Chomsky and the Chomskian paradigm in constructing a critique of what can only be referred to as vulgar correlationalism, though it passes for "Sociolinguistics", at least in North America. Chomsky himself deals fairly explicitly with what he calls Orwell's problem, the problem, in essence, of how evidence is ignored and how people end up buying propaganda and subscribing to the consent manufactured for them. In light of this, it is, I believe, incumbent upon me to reflect, with you, on what has hitherto been used only as a counterpoint. What I want to do in this lecture, then, is to look at how Chomsky views the connection between what he calls Plato's Problem, best illustrated according to him, by language, and Orwell's Problem (cf. Chomsky 1980).

Plato's Problem, in essence, is the problem of how knowledge that goes far beyond evidence is possible; Orwell's Problem, on the other hand, is the problem of how and why evidence is systematically ignored. Unlike some contemporary linguists, who are busy planting trees in Plato's Problem without paying much attention to what the forest may look like, Chomsky knows it well.

Perhaps the best place to begin, exploring the distinctions he makes, is his two Managua lectures: *Language and Problems of Knowledge (LPK)* and *On Power and Ideology (OPI)*. Together they raise an enormous number of issues, and no one can do justice to them all. All I can do is to outline what is in those books, and take up some of the issues that seem important to me.

LPK is, primarily, a non-technical, or minimally technical, expansion of Chomsky's well-known argument that, under standard assumptions of learning, language is essentially unlearnable. The miracle of language acquisition, he argues, requires some version of time-and-space independent hard-wiring (*à la* Plato and Descartes) of the human species. Language, according to him, is the best window on Plato's problem... our best chance to guess precisely what we as humans bring to bear on the data we are exposed to. *LPK* provides a thumb-nail sketch of Platonist (or mentalist) attempts to deal with Plato's Problem and places Chomskian linguistics within the context of those efforts.

Committed to the view that a substantial part of knowledge of language comes, in Hume's phrase, "from the original hand of nature", Chomsky devotes a substantial part of *LPK* (chapters 2,3, and 4) to outlining what he sees as the nature and structure of that prespecified knowledge, illustrating his hypotheses with examples from Spanish. Some of the main ingredients of this prespecified contribution from the hand of nature are captured with the notions of structure dependence, binding theory, and the empty category principle. These ingredients function, according to Chomsky, exactly like "chemical elements, molecules" and "other constructs of science", and "we can look forward to the discovery of physical mechanisms that have the properties brought to light in this inquiry" (p. 90).

The relatively heavy prespecification of the human language faculty proposed by Chomsky would lead one to expect one human language with perhaps multiple lexica, but the challenge of variation should, according to him, be met neither by ignoring the obvious fact that languages plainly differ nor by giving in to variationism of the vulgar kind (cf. Chomsky 1980). It cannot, at any rate, be met by variationism of the sort, espoused by, for example, Labov (cf. Singh and Ford 1980). It is to be met, Chomsky believes, by leaving certain parameters of this prespecified knowledge open and by having them "fixed by experience in one or another way" (p.62). He suggests the following metaphor:

> We may think of the language faculty as a complex and intricate network of some sort associated with a switch box consisting of an array of switches that can be in one of two positions. Unless the switches are set one way or another, the system does not function.

> When they are set in one of the permissible ways, then the system functions in accordance with its nature, but differently, depending on how the switches are set. The fixed network is the system of principles of universal grammar: the switches are the parameters to be fixed by experience. The data presented to the child learning the langauge must suffice to set the switches one way or another. When these switches are set, the child has command of a particular language and knows the facts of that language: that a particular expression has a particular meaning, and so on. (pp. 62-63)

If the logic of the situation were not something like that, it would, Chomsky argues, not be possible for the child to learn any given language (p. 65). The entire discussion regarding the human language faculty is succinctly summarized by him towards the end of chapter 4:

> Throughout the discussion we find illustrations of Plato's problem, illustrations that become more complex as we proceed. The person who has mastered any human language has developed a system of knowledge that is rich and complex. This cognitive system provides specific and precise knowledge of many intricate and surprising facts. It seems that the mind carries out precise computational operations, using mental representations of a specific form to arrive at precise conclusions about factual matters of no little complexity, without conscious thought or deliberation. The principles that determine the nature of mental representation and the operations that apply to them form a central part of our biologically determined nature. They constitute the human language faculty, which one might regard as an 'organ of the mind/brain.' As inquiry reveals its often surprising properties, we become better able to approach Plato's problem and to solve it and also to understand, in part at least, how we are capable of using language in normal life in the manner that we do, though Descartes's problem, the problem posed by the creative aspect of language use, still remains to be addressed. (p.131)

The last chapter of *LPK* sketches out the prospects for the study of mind as Chomsky sees them. The chapter opens with the slightly reworded versions of questions with which *LPK* begins and takes us, step by step, to the implications their putative answers have for the study of mind, via the familiar exposé of the absurdity of poor behaviourist theories of language (pp. 137-130). Most of it is devoted to a discussion of Descartes' problem, the problem posed by the creative aspect of language use (p. 136). The issues of creative use of language arose in the context of the mind-body problem and forced Cartesians to postulate *res cogitans*, a substance entirely separate from the body and not subject to mechanical explanations in terms of Cartesian contact mechanics. Newtonian physics rendered the Cartesian account of the body untenable, and that, according to Chomsky, leaves us free to solve the problem at hand by adopting the doctrine that "any intelligible theory that offers genuine explanations and that can be assimilated to the core notions of physics becomes a part of the theory of the material world, part of our account of body" (p. 144). Chomsky, thus, proposes assimilating the Cartesian mind to the Newtonian body without necessarily giving up what, he argues, can be achieved by construing the study of mind as "a study of the abstract properties of brain mechanisms" (p. 8).

Devoted according to Chomsky to helping us "comprehend the meaning and truth of Simon Bolivar's statement, over 150 years ago, that the United States seems destined to plague and torment the continent in the name of freedom" (p.3), *OPI* is made up of the five afternoon lectures Chomsky gave in Managua the same week he gave the lectures that make up LPK. OPI is an attempt to sketch out what he sees as the "persistent and largely invariant features of U.S. foreign policy", correlating them to "U.S. institutions" and to "the distribution of power in the domestic society of the United States" (p. 5).

The first lecture ("The overall framework of order") presents myth-exploding paraphrases of what he considers to be "democracy", "freedom of speech", "anti-imperialism" and "open door". It is primarily an exposé of the nature and structure of the propaganda machine by which American power seeks to legitimatize itself.

The second lecture, "Containing internal aggression", is devoted mainly to a detailed discussion of the two versions of the domino theory — the internal "that consistently guides planning" and the external that is "designed to frighten the population" (p.39). The third lecture, entitled "Our little region over here", gets to matters closer to home for his Managua audience. It is devoted to a detailed account of the human rights violations in El Salvador and Guatemala, to U.S. commitments to terrorist operations in Central America, to empirically rich details of what Chomsky infers must be the correct answer to the question: "What is a Castro?" and to some major and minor successes of the American system of indoctrination. It also provides a thoughtful answer to the question: "Why do imperial powers seek to control empires even when it involves, or seems to involve, costs?": the costs are only social but the benefits are private (p. 75). "The empire", he notes, "is just one of the many devices by which the poor subsidize the wealthy in the home society" (p.75).

In "National security policy", the penultimate lecture, Chomsky turns his attention to "national security policy, the arms race, and the threat of nuclear war" (p.91). That the national leadership of the United States "has always regarded the use of nuclear weapons as a live policy" is, Chomsky argues, more than borne out by the fact that the Blechman-Kaplan study documents 19 cases between 1946 and 1973 "when the U.S. deployed strategic weapons or placed them on alert, ready for use" (p. 91). As far as "defense" is concerned, Chomsky sums up his analysis of the empty rhetoric of defense as follows: "If we had records we would probably discover that Attilathe Hun was acting in self-defense" (p. 99). The reasons for the arms race and what it may involve are, Chomsky argues, institutional, and "the problems must be confronted without illusions" (p. 110).

In "The domestic scene", the last lecture, Chomsky returns to the internal dynamics of American society to consider precisely what makes it destined to do what Bolivar claimed it is bound to. He comments, often tellingly, on the now familiar structures and institutions of pluralist democracies: after all, as the first Chief Justice of the U.S. Supreme Court held, "the people who own the country ought to govern it" (p. 117). What is advertised as democracy is, Chomsky contends, really only the freedom to settle within a shared consensus sometimes conflicting interests of various segments of business (p. 115).

As should be obvious from the brief summaries just provided, *LPK* and *OPI* raise an extremely large range of issues. It is perhaps convenient to divide them into two major categories — internal and external. I shall comment on the internal, descriptive issues only briefly, because it is clear that a minor difference in the facts of the matter would make no difference to Chomsky's conclusions. I shall take up the books in the order in which I have just summarized them.

LPK presents both descriptive and explanatory problems that deserve some comment. The first of these has to do with the fact that although Chomsky admits the possibility that the number faculty is still dormant and unused in several human groups (p.16), he dismisses that possibility as far as language is concerned as "a biological miracle" (p. 38) and offers only functionalist arguments. One would, however, like to know why this difference exists, and if it is generally true of secondary functions of genetically selected Darwinian advantages.

Chomsky's contention that "the child unerringly selects the computationally more complex structure-dependent rules" (p. 48) also presents a bit of a problem, for the available evidence (cf. Felix 1988) seems to suggest that the child does, in fact, violate principles of Universal Grammar (UG) en route to selecting the computationally complex structure-dependent rules. The way out of this would seem to be either the Katzian position that the complexity in question is a property of language that the child discovers and not something s/he brings to it, or the maturationist position that the only principles that can be violated at any given point are those that the maturation schedule has not "released". The maturation hypothesis is an attractive one, but it is not clear in what way it provides a better account of the matter, and the Katzian alternative would appear to be unacceptable to Chomsky.

The example of artificially constructed languages used by Chomsky would also appear to present some problems. He claims that these would be harder to learn (pp. 46-47) and they would be learned by "other faculties of the mind" (p. 26). He may well be right, but there is precious little on the acquisition of artificially constructed languages and it is not easy to see precisely how one could show that the human language faculty can't be involved in acquiring them. Again, the point is not that Chomsky's position is not tenable, but merely that the conclusion follows from definitional considerations, and is not "independently" supported.

The parametric interpretation of traditional typological concerns of linguistics Chomsky provides gives linguists powerful conceptual tools with which to make sense of the anarchy of vulgar variationism, but it is not clear yet precisely what the limits of the parametric enterprise are and if the correlational consistency the model proposes actually obtains. In a large number of cases, it seems not to hold any better than the traditional notion "typologically consistent". And the extent to which parametric settings involve left/right settings, and the explanatory potential of parameters would seem to be undermined by the fact that the linearity of language doesn't really permit any other choice. In the context of public lectures such as LPK, the faith Chomsky puts in parameters is, of course, justified, but even there I wish it had been appropriately qualified.

These are all, however, descriptive issues that deserve and get greater attention from Chomsky and his students in work that is considered "linguistics proper" by a large segment of the community of linguists.

OPI is, as should be obvious from its summary, a descriptively rich book, for Chomsky provides detailed accounts of policy and policy-making, citing sources that are all there to see and consult except for the Orwellian curtain drawn over them. The reality that leaks through carefully worded and cautiously presented policy is captured by Chomsky with an unerring eye.

But one may legitimately wonder why Chomsky generally leaves his commentary on American foreign policy on the level of ironic anger against the individual actors and policy-dictators, -makers, and -executioners and why sometimes his assumptions don't seem very different from those of his targets. Consider, for example, his separation between "investment decisions" and "political decisions". The former, he says, "have to do with what is produced, how it is produced, and what work is done, how production and profits are distributed and to whom"; the latter, with "which groups actually participate" in shaping state policy (p.116). One would have thought that the main thrust of Chomsky's demonstration was that the putative political autonomy attributed to the second category was a myth.

Chomsky's *real-politik* critiques are "articulate ironic expressions of outrage", but they seem to get to neither history nor to the abstract principles he thinks he is after, and the tradition he believes he is a part of WAS constantly after.

One wishes that Chomsky had chosen to analyze rather than just describe the facts of the matter even according to his own logic. Consider, for example, his observation that there is no correlation between "the internal freedom of some society and its external violence and repression" (p. 114). I am sure that if Chomsky had the time, he would have drawn the audience's attention to the facts that under colonialism there is in fact a strong negative correlation and that violence and repression are used not only with alien subjects but with those segments of the native population unable to buy a sufficient number of shares in the stock called Freedom.

Equally inescapable seems to be the fact that although Chomsky rightly ridicules the elitist view that the masses are ignorant and understand nothing (p. 153), he doesn't offer many insights into precisely how they repeatedly show that they are not. The passing ironic reference to their unfortunate tendency to succumb to unacceptable ideas shows that he believes that they are not, but he focuses not on the subaltern assertions of their rationality but on the manipulators of the dis-information system. It is obvious that these manipulators don't really believe the doctrine that the masses are stupid: if they were, there would be no need for the commissars to be constantly on the run, manufacturing consent after consent, ideology after ideology, no need to discover subtler and subtler mechanisms of indoctrination. Equally obvious seems to be the fact that these idealogies are "bought" by the masses not because they are stupid but because they see them as containing a truth that haunts from within the lies manufactured by the commissars. The success of ideologies, in other word, seems to call for something more than what Chomsky offers. HIS logic should lead him to argue that the people of his state collaborate with the appropriators not by default and not because they can't see what is all around them but because of their deep-rooted instrumentalism.

Again, the point is not that this deep-rooted instrumentalism exists, but that Chomsky does not pursue the logic of his demonstrations and somewhat unwarrantedly draws the conclusions he does from the point where he stops, somewhat arbitrarily.

Finally, I believe one is entitled to ask that if things are the way Chomsky says they are, why doesn't he reflect on the conclusion his logic should lead him to: the conclusion, that is, that the flow of critical impulses such as Chomsky's is built into the system he is being critical of. To put it humorously, one might say that the system he critiques needs him just as *NLLT* needed Pullum! Critical theorists have actually long insisted that the flow of critical impulses has to be guaranteed to appropriate the surplus back from them in order to sustain a slightly modified version of what the critique was a critique of. I emphasize that I am not saying that this is right, but simply that I find it puzzling that Chomsky does not reflect on that possibility.

Chomsky's analysis of American politics, in other words, is a critique of instrumentalism, as practised by the rulers. It arises out of a moral anger which we share, but what is missing is the analysis of the processes that systematically inculcate that instrumentalism as a virtue among the citizens, such that they become and remain willing and even vocal allies of their rulers in the systematic perpetration of what Chomsky doesn't like. What are we to make of the fact that such violence is always justified in the name of freedom, human rights, or as a fight against the "evil", "faithless" or "communist" empires? Whereas Ronald Reagan used to draw crowds as "the Great Communicator", why do Chomskyan demystifications remain cloistered in a discourse shared only by a minuscule minority? Can this be simply a matter of telling a lie a thousand times, whereby it comes to be believed as truth? Are not the citizens, like native speakers, in the domain of language, supposed to be both rational and creative? Why then do they systematically misunderstand, misinterpret and "misintuit" rational signals that abound even within the lies and justifications that are routinely communicated to them?

It is legitimate to ask: "What are the links between these two books?"Perhaps the best way to begin a discussion of these links is to see how Chomsky views them himself. He views his politics as a matter of hopes, aspirations and intuitions; his analysis of mechanisms of indoctrination as a matter of trivial scientific understanding; and his analyses and hypotheses in linguistics as a matter of "substantial scientific understanding" (*LPK*: 195). Although he very briefly alludes, towards the end of *LPK*, to the possibility that the last two enterprises "may have something to do with one another" (p.195), he is generally reluctant to give the former the status of serious "science" because it seems not to be able to generate "technically" complex principles such as "binding" or "cycle".

There are various possibilities: (i) Chomsky's politics is a matter of rationality and "science" and not a matter of his hopes and aspirations; (ii) Chomsky's linguistics is a matter of his personal experience, hopes, and aspirations and not a matter of rationality and "science"; (iii) the Chomskyan dichotomy Plato's Problem/Orwell's Problem is valid only because the latter is not taken seriously by him; and (iv) he is correct in separating his politics from Orwell's Problem and hence his linguistics and politics shall never meet.

I would like to consider the possibility that given what he says, the separations are not as clear-cut as Chomsky thinks they are. He himself provides several arguments in *LPK* and *OPI* that, on the one hand, provide a firmer grounding for linking his politics to Orwell's problem, and, on the other, somewhat undermine the time-space independence of his solutions to the aspects of Plato's Problem he discusses. Consider, for example, the following passage from *LPK*:

> "The same is true of moral judgement. What its basis may be we do not know, but we can hardly doubt that it is rooted in fundamental human nature. It cannot be merely a matter of convention that we find some things to be right, others wrong. Growing up in a particular society, a child acquires standards and principles of moral judgement. These are acquired on the basis of limited evidence, but they have broad and often quite precise applicability. It is often though not always true that people can discover or be convinced that their judgements about a particular case are wrong, in the sense that the judgements are inconsistent with the person's own internalized principles. Moral argument is not always pointless, merely a matter of 'I assert this' and 'you assert that'. The acquisition of a specific moral and ethical system, wide ranging and often precise in its consequences, cannot simply be the result of 'shaping' and 'control' by the social environment. As in the case of language, the environment is far too impoverished and indeterminate to provide this system to the child, in its full richness and applicability. Knowing little about the matter, we are compelled to speculate; but it certainly seems reasonable to speculate that the moral and ethical system acquired by the child owes much to some innate human faculty. The environment is relevant, as in the case of language, vision, and so on; thus we can find individual and cultural divergence. But there is surely a common basis, rooted in our nature." (pp. 152-153)

The extent to which moral judgements are "acquired on the basis of limited evidence" and the extent to which the capacity to formulate them is rooted in "fundamental human nature" is the extent to which Chomsky's critique of the mechanisms of indoctrination, exemplified in *OPI*, is a contribution to our understanding of Plato's problem. The two problems, in other words, are not as separate or separable as Chomsky thinks they are, unfortunately weakening his own case. His analysis of Orwell's problem is grounded in the same place as his analysis of Plato's problem, or so it would appear.

The political behaviour of people seems to suggest the same underlying rationality that the Enlightenment philosophers based their case on. Consider the following observation in *OPI*:

> "The major enemy, however, is always the indigenous population, which has an unfortunate tendency to succumb to strange and unacceptable ideas about using their resources for their own purposes. They must therefore be taught regular lessons in obedience to thwart any such evil designs." (p.9)

The "unfortunate tendency" Chomsky refers to follows from "the laws of our nature" and reveals, repeatedly and with enriched new sense, that Truth, Freedom and Justice are not utopian fantasies but the fundamental predicates of human existence. Chomsky shows a keen awareness of the rationality hidden behind this tendency but is, like us all, constrained (for reasons sketched out in Lele and Singh 1989). Even when he is right, he misses Weberian pathos, to examine the discourses of the privileged, and thereby ends up in believing that his attempts to comprehend Orwell's problem are not a matter of "substantial scientific understanding". By HIS logic, they are, for his own work repeatedly demonstrates the existence of what one is tempted to call the moral and political organs.

Although he is, as the following passage from *LPK* shows, aware of the fact that the predecessors he regards as his did not make the distinction, he suspends it only when discussing the intellectual tradition he is legitimately a distinguished part of:

> "In discussing the intellectual tradition in which I believe contemporary work finds its natural place, I do not make a sharp

> distinction between philosophy and science. The distinction, justifiable or not, is a fairly recent one. In dealing with the topics that concern us here, traditional thinkers did not regard themselves as 'philosophers' as distinct from 'scientists'. Descartes, for example, was one of the leading scientists of his day. What we call his 'philosophical work' is not separable from his 'scientific work' but is rather a component of it concerned with the conceptual foundations of science and the outer reaches of scientific speculation and (in his eyes) inference. David Hume, in his inquiries into human thought, considered his project to be akin to Newton's. He aimed to discover the elements of human nature and the principles that enter into and guide our mental life. The term 'philosophy' was used to include what we would call science, so that physics was called natural philosophy and the term 'philosophical grammar' meant scientific grammar." (p. 2)

The truth that seems to "leak through" (*OPI*: 108) this passage is that Chomsky is somewhat ambivalent about the distinction science/ philosophy. This "fairly recent" distinction is precisely the one he makes when he distinguishes amongst his contributions to our understanding of what he calls Plato's Problem, Orwell's Problem and politics. His not making that distinction "in discussing the intellectual tradition in which I believe contemporary work finds its natural place" is a civilized, sophisticated, and sensitive overture to the past, but his making it elsewhere, actually throughout *LPK*, is indicative of his belief that it IS justified.

That justification is formulated as follows in the concluding section of *LPK*:

> "In the realm of social thought we don't really have good evidence for anything, so our conceptions are more an expression of our hopes and our intuitive judgements and our personal experience and the ways we understand history than they are the product of any substantial scientific understanding. My own personal commitments and hopes are more or less of the sort that I described: that is, they are based on the ideas of libertarian socialism, that is, rooted in some of the ideas of Rousseau, Humboldt, Marx, Bakunin, and others, with a crucial concern for the opportunity for meaningful creative work under the control of the workers. Here I would understand work in a very broad sense, and in fact, I would consider that these ideas extend to control over every other aspect of social and personal life." (p. 195)

It is surprising to see the demonstrations of Marx, Gramsci, Habermas and various others, including the author of *OPI*, dismissed as not providing evidence for anything. Chomsky seems to seriously undermine his own demonstrations and the evidence available from the laboratory called human history. His modesty here seems somewhat misplaced.

He does, however, indicate that there is a vague, ever so uncapturable, connection and that perhaps the tradition he represents was right in not making the distinction he almost seems to insist on!

> "Well, do these two concepts have anything to do with one another? They may. It could be that there's a connection between the creative aspect of language use, which is part of the human essence, part of what Marx called the species character of the human being (the character of the species); there may be a connection between that and the idea of a distinctly human need for productive and creative work (including intellectual work) under one's own control, that is, control of producers over production, which is the essence of Marxist thought, among other intellectual traditions. So there may be a connection between these two things. They're conceptually rather similar, and that connection, if it holds, if it is real, which it may well be, is independent of victories and defeats in imperialist wars." (pp. 175-196)

The qualifications and hedges, undoubtedly honest, that he introduces in the passage above seem to result from the methodological limitation that makes it impossible for us all to enter into a dialogue with the unprivileged. In linguistics, he not only speaks on behalf of the native speaker, he also speaks as one; in politics, he only speaks on behalf of the naive citizen, again like us all so-called intellectuals. We have all lost the ability to hear those on whose behalf we claim to speak, and they know this because they suspect us as much as those we criticize. What makes Chomsky so effective is his awareness, often expressed as irony, of the fact that some of us have turned our deafness into an "advantage" by accepting the role of "ideological managers".

Turning our attention to the other side of the coin, we find that Chomsky not only makes the distinction that was not made by those whose modern heir he legitimately claims to be, but also accepts the folklore about science somewhat uncritically and puts his faith in the contemporary scientistic abridgement of Reason. That he may well be aware of this difference is shown by passages like the following, strewn with adjectives that seem to argue too hard:

> "Rather, we are studying the properties of the material world at a level of abstraction at which we believe, rightly or wrongly, that a GENUINE EXPLANATORY theory can be constructed, a theory that provides GENUINE INSIGHT into the nature of the phenomena that concern us. These phenomena, in fact are of REAL intellectual interest not so much in themselves but in the avenue that they provide for us to PENETRATE INTO THE DEEPER WORKINGS OF THE MIND. Ultimately, we hope to assimilate this study to the mainstream of the natural science, much as the study of genes or of valence and the properties of the chemical elements was assimilated to more fundamental sciences." (p. 145—emphasis mine)

Although he admits the possibility "that the concepts of the physical sciences might have to be modified" (*LPK*: 145), he takes the core notions of physics to be the results of a happy convergence between our science-forming capacity and truth (*LPK*: 158). Despite an occasional concession of this sort, his view of science is, surprisingly, folkloristic.

Chomsky's view that his politics is largely a matter of hopes and aspirations and not of scientific understanding, notwithstanding the evidence he himself provides, cannot be properly understood without counterpointing it against his view that such is not the case with what we all call science. Although he allows for the possibility that the core concepts of science may have be modified and extended, he shows a surprisingly unusual faith in the cumulative character of scientific discoveries: he doesn't reflect on the ontological status of these core concepts and does not seem to even recognize that since the 17th century the instrumental abridgement of Reason that leads to "science" has systematically eroded the moral dimension of curiosity, grounded in the human instinct for survival. The 17th century is, according to the tradition which he says he belongs to, less a matter of the happy coincidence between truth and our science-forming faculty and more a matter of the entrenchment of the equation: will to knowledge = will to power (cf. Gadamer 1981: 155 ff.).

Chomsky's model of modifications in the physical sciences, and, by extension, in linguistics, relies on what he calls "puzzling questions".

The naive faith which Chomsky shows in the innocent genesis of these "puzzles" cannot, unfortunately, be taken seriously from the author of *OPI*. How do puzzling questions arise, or not arise? There is, it should be obvious, a naive separation in Chomsky between will to know and will to power. In fact, as far as knowledge is concerned, there seems no place for will, only an organic propensity to discover. Will comes into play only when "false" ideas about "reality" are perpetuated: ideas that "are not simply in error but entirely beyond any hope of repair" (*LPK*: 137). The questions he finds interesting regarding these false ideas — how they are proposed, how they are sustained as "the leading ideas" and how their critiques are ignored or silenced — seem equally relevant to all scientific theories. The generative enterprise, even if completely "true", is maintained, has to be maintained, in exactly the ways in which Chomsky suggests, and rightly, that these false ideas were. The success of the generative enterprise owes as much to the fundamentally correct, or corrective, insights of Chomsky as to a fairly efficient management by its "ideological managers".

Chomsky seems to be aware of the absence of a secure ground for his faith because words like "genuine insight" appear rather frequently in his defence of his linguistic enterprise. He keeps pleading for continued efforts to penetrate into the "deeper workings of the mind" and for assimilation to the "main-stream" of the natural sciences, as they are themselves being "modified" and "extended". The source of this faith is supposed to be: "the method of rational inquiry". It seems to imply some spontaneous overflow of curiosity that goes beyond the humdrum redundancy ("common sense") of everyday life (as a special quality of those with a mature scientific organ, an individual genius, one might ask?) to raise questions that cannot be answered by a given theory (that was, says Chomsky, once a startling new discovery in response to similar questions, but has now become humdrum common sense). With increasing abstractions, we move farther and farther away from the authentic, creative everyday activity of the native speaker. If we follow Arbib and Hesse (1986) we also move away from domains or theories far removed from the original empirical base (such as fundamental physics, today). Here, scientific theories make massive extrapolations and have characteristics similar to those of myths. And the ghost of Orwell haunts not only the corridors of the history of science — how else does a Marconi get all the credit for short-wave radio? or, questions of nuclear fission become THE questions of today's science? — but also the very foundations on which Chomsky builds the case for his Cartesian solution, purged of the error of *res cogitans*, to Plato's problem.

Chomsky separates the "creative use" of language (with its aesthetic value produced by poets, novelists, special stylists) from "the ordinary use of language in everyday life". The latter he says has its own distinctive properties: novelty, freedom, coherence, appropriateness and a capacity to evoke appropriate thoughts in the listeners. In a sense, this shows an awareness of the poetic-authentic, spontaneous dimension of everyday speech, but without a sense for the negative dimension, the embedded repression that can also produce appropriateness of various sorts, giving only an appearance of authenticity. And, in the final analysis, it is ironic that the world's best known Cartesian linguist has precious little to say about what he himself refers to as the Descarte's problem.

Questions such as these lead to the established tradition of the ideology critique, enlarged and deepened by its encounters with phenomenology. When we translate some elements of Chomsky's theory of language along the lines suggested by that tradition, which, I remind you, is the tradition HE says he is a part of, we may still understand the language faculty as securely grounded in our bodily nature. However, as such, it can also become the source of a critique of distortion. One might, with some exaggeration, say that an ungrammatical sentence HURTS a native speaker's ear in a way similar to the hurt caused by a false musical note, or by physical atrocities committed against oneself or other innocent human beings. In an analogous way, one may suggest that the knowledge of what should be a practically correct (in the classical sense of "moral-practical") political action is also deeply rooted in our bodies. In both cases, however, that bodily-grounded knowledge BECOMES human only when it is brought to life in relationship with other human beings. The "Great Communicators" seem to know this in a way that the theorists of language and society do not. That is why justifications of oppressive, inhuman practices always promise joy, autonomy (or serenity) and an end to suffering, for individuals and communities.

One may legitimately ask what possible steps could plausibly lead to a theoretical synthesis of linguistics and politics. Perhaps the initial step would have to be the replacement of the view that learning a language is largely a passive unfolding of the hard-wired program of UG with the view that it is a creative confrontation between the child's natural-social predisposition and the socially encrusted system presented to him as his language (cf. Singh, forthcoming). One may also have to redefine competence as the linguistic potential of the speaker rather than as the system underlying the production/perception of what is called his language. The standard view that a speaker is merely a derivative extension of the principles that generative grammarians have postulated, to describe what they call his language, would have to be given up in favour of the *point de départ* that sees the speaker as both larger and smaller than his "language": larger because he can change it and smaller because it may provide him with the potential his place in society may have denied him (cf. Singh 1996b).

Although Chomsky sees his work as dealing with only two problems, it should be obvious that he has three projects. First, there is the structuralist project along empiricist-rationalist lines of theorising from minimum empirical evidence with the final appeal to the falsifiability criterion along with an anarchy of language specific rules that cannot be comprehensively or logically integrated at the level of general principles. The second one is based on the assumption that, despite dramatic paradigmatic changes, the "core concepts" of physics are "well established" and the linguist, by mapping the basic principles of language faculty, can help the discovery of associated neural mechanisms of the brain. The plea is not incompatible with any structuralist enterprise and although its logic is clear, its empirical dimensions still need to be fleshed out. Third, there is the political, critical project, which includes what Chomsky calls Orwell's Problem. Chomsky sees the connection between the first two as more solid than it might be and the connection between the last two as weaker than on closer analysis it turns out to be, again according to his own logic. The perceived solidity of the first connection derives from logical considerations and his faith in structural linguistics of the type he advocated and from practices providing to biology what 19th century chemistry provided to physics, and in what he takes modern science to be. His attempt to transform what has generally been regarded as a cloud into a clock (cf. Popper and Eccles 1977: 34) is probably what leads him to think that the second connection is an entirely different kettle of fish.

Although not unaware of the fact that there is a connection between language and politics, Chomsky, given his other commitments and his other priorities, seems UNABLE to let the twain meet. In insisting that there is only a vague connection between his linguistics and his political ideas, he is in fact being very accurate, for he cannot maintain his political ideas as a matter of scientific, rational belief without modifying his linguistics. And given his maximalist linguistics despite recent minimalist overtures, he HAS to keep the two apart. Given the fact that he has confidence in the Newtonization of linguistics, he cannot but be content with modest claims on behalf of his discussion of Orwell's Problem. And in doing so, he seems to undermine the possibility of a sociolinguistics in which the native speaker can legitimately claim her sovereign right to rationality and her language.

12. STATISTICS AND THE STRUCTURE OF LANGUAGE

I am not just
A handful of atoms.
I am nobody's
Quantum or quark.
I will never give up
Asking questions.
I refuse to believe
In the dark.

P. Stratford 1992: 57

The relevance/irrelevance of statistics to the structure of language raises the question of whether statistics furnishes an appropriate meta-language for linguistics, and by implication, for other social and human sciences, its caveats regarding nominal, non-parametric and ordinal etc. and regarding "what is worth investigating" notwithstanding.

I shall plead that, for some very well-grounded reasons, the structure of language is not amenable to statistics and that it actually provides some reason to doubt not only the regulative interpretation of constitutiveness imposed by statistics, but also the correspondence theory of truth on which statistics, like other branches of mathematics, is based.

I should perhaps begin with a few simple illustrations of what typical textbooks designed to teach statistical methods to linguists and other social scientists construe as matters of language. I must, however, make it clear that it is not my intention to ridicule the authors of the manuals from which I shall draw my examples. They are merely doing what someone else would have done if they had decided not to do it. Perhaps the best-known manuals of the sort I am talking about are Butler (1985) and Hatch and Farhady (1982). Butler contains pretty silly exercises like asking students to calculate the Spearman correlation coefficient for the responses provided by 10-year-old English-speaking children and their teachers, asked to rank a few passages of English according to the degree of difficulty felt by the children and imagined on their behalf by their teachers. Irrespective of what we can learn about the historical development of the notion of difficulty chez homo sapiens, the exercise cannot possibly reveal anything about English, or any other natural language. Hatch and Farhady contains examples galore that have more to do with impressing school-boards and granting agencies than with language. Although I do not mean to belittle their useful book, I must report that I could not find a single example in it that I could interpret as having to do with the structure of language.

I do not want to waste your time with textbooks. Besides, textbook writers should not be faulted for producing what the market-place seems to require. I shall, therefore, turn to a real book, written, this time, by a statistician. Brainerd (1974) is, apparently, meant to show how applied statistics can help us in our study of language.

After a good, solid introduction to various statistical techniques and measures, Brainerd gets down to the business of applying these to the study of language in the last chapter of his book, and the examples are interesting. The first has to do with the use of the article in English. After bemoaning the fact that there has been very little sampling theory developed for the mean of a Poisson variate, he takes us through Bartlett's test for equal variance and Scheffe's test to conclude that although article usage may be genre-specific it is not author-specific. Even this conclusion is arrived at with multiple reliance on the native-speaker's nose. *The Wapshot Chronicle* is, we are told, "anomalous" because "it is a mixture of different types of writing" (223). The type of writing, curiously enough, is defined in terms of an article-use average.

This study is followed by a consideration of pronouns versus articles. The finding that the number of articles is inversely correlated with the number of pronouns across textual blocs can only make a linguist smile because of Postal's (1969) classic paper called "On so called 'pronouns' in English" and because of the mutual exclusivity of these categories forthrightly suggested by the ungrammaticality of such English expressions as **the my house*. What makes the smile even broader is Brainerd's decision to discard the entries from Joseph Conrad "on the grounds that Conrad, not being a native-speaker of English, will have an anomalous style" (238). I shall ignore thousands of native-speakers of English I would trade for a Conrad and draw your attention to Cavell's (1958) classic reply to Mates (1958): if the native-speaker cannot count on his own nose, there would be nothing to count (p. 78). Or, as Austin (1956) would have put it, "It is not enough to show how clever we are by showing how obscure everything is."

Brainerd, in his next study, argues that "a reasonable case can be made for the hypothesis that the frequencies of syllables per word follow the negative binomial distribution" (248) except for things like *Time*, *The Lady of the Lake*, and *Henry IV* for which he invokes mysterious things like heterogeneity and poetical form. Maybe the case in question can be made, but what possible interest could that have? The syllable-density per word follows from whether or not you speak what Dasgupta (1993) calls the Parisian dialect of English.

Brainerd's explorations also take him to phonology. In that domain, he tells us, the filling of phonemic slots from the phonemic alphabets of two languages can be construed as "a sequence of Bernouilli trials" (257), under the assumption that the choice for each slot is independent of the other choices. It may be so construed, but, the linguist smiles again: why would you do so, given that phonology is essentially a study of the lack of choice in phonemic combinatorics, albeit mathematically elementary?

Brainerd's book, he says, is intended as "an introduction to the fundamental notions of classical statistics and probability theory that have application in the study of language" (265). The problem is that the notions he so clearly and elegantly introduces do not seem to have any applications. Perhaps I am not being fair. Let us look at what are generally claimed to be the triumphs of applied statistics in language-studies (1) phonological variability and (2) address-systems.

One of the major triumphs of applied statistics for linguistics is supposed to be what Rousseau and Sankoff (1978) call the study of optional rule application from a probabilistic point of view. The problem studied is what is called phonological variability, the model used is the logistic model most generally used for the analysis of binary data (Jones 1975 and Lindsey 1975), and the analysis consists of multiple regression analysis in order, as Rousseau (1989: 396) puts it, "to explain variant choice as a function of the linguistic and/or extralinguistic context of the variable." Some allowance is made for knock-outs and heterogenous partitions. In the typical multivariant case, multinomial analysis is said to yield "estimates of the effect of each factor on the probability of occurrence for each variant" (Rousseau 1989: 403).

Now, all this is presumably impressive, statistically that is. But is there any need for it anywhere? And does it explain anything? Let us consider the classical case of word-final consonant deletion. The phenomenon has been studied extensively by, amongst others, Guy (1980), Labov (1971 and 1987), Terrell (1977) and Tranel (1976). Labov proposes the following variable rule of word-final consonant deletion:

(1) [+ cons] → <Ø> / <[+ cons]> <Ø> __ <# #> <[- sy]>

His interpretation of (1) reads as follows:

(2) "The rule asserts that whenever a final consonant is variably deleted the rule will operate more often if another consonant precedes it, if it is an integral part of the word and not a separate morpheme, and if it is not followed by a word beginning with a vowel" (1971: 272-73).

The advance here is supposed to be the statistical computation of the probability of deletion under the variable conditions enumerated by Labov. The computation proceeds as outlined by Rousseau and Sankoff and various others. It is difficult to see for whom these estimates of the effect of each factor on the probability of occurrence may be useful: certainly not for the speaker who only needs to know their relative influence and not the raw probability figures. That relative ordering can, however, be predicted by other, non-statistical means, but that requires another set of questions. The right questions to ask regarding (1), it seems to me, are: (i) why should the deletion depend on (a) a preceding consonant, (b) a following vowel, and (c) the lexical/grammatical status of the segment in question? and (ii) what is common between the phonological variables (a) and (b)? Suppose the rule is not what Labov says it is and that what it really does is to reduce moras (defined tentatively as number of segments in the rime). Now a VCC rime (3 moras) can be reduced to a 2 mora rime either by deleting the final C or by syllabifying it with the vowel to its right if there is one. If what is to its right is a C, it would predictably be far more difficult to achieve this mora-reduction (the onset possibilities in the language will play a crucial role). Substantive constraints on possible onsets of the type discussed in Singh (1980) and obvious to anyone who has ever seen or worked with sanskrit sandhi rules tell us that the putative target of deletion is more likely to form a possible complex onset with a liquid than with another obstruent. Is it surprising, then, to find that Guy offers the following refinement of (b): consonant > liquid > vowel?

As far as explanation is concerned, it should be obvious that irrespective of how many variables one isolates and how sophisticated a statistical analysis one performs, the metalanguage furnished by probability cannot explain why this variability has the structure it has, and that once you know the metrical and rhythmic principles of prosodic organization, you can more or less predict the relevant part of what applied statistical methods can only tortuously compute. The fact that a multivariate analysis can be very useful for someone who does not know anything about the structure of human language or rhythm is, I'm afraid, a poor excuse for wanting to universalize what must in this case be called, despite its heuristic value, the metalanguage of ignorance. The problem is that even when we are invited to consider some factors as knock-outs, the applied statistician is reluctant to consider the possibility that there is nothing else but knock-outs in language. The somewhat odd mixture of apples and oranges he calls variability is his construct, and the positivistic joy he is able to derive from analyzing, it is of no consequence either to speakers or to linguists, for phonologies have only categorical rules. They appear variable only when one does not understand the nature of the higher level prosodic principles that regulate this apparent variability. The heuristic value of the tools furnished by statistics, particularly in discovering clusterings and subtle influences that may on more informal observation be hard to detect, is, I repeat, not in doubt. It is hard, though, to reconcile Sankoff's reminder, repeated by Labov (1980: xiv), that multivariate analysis and probability theory presuppose an algebra not only with Labov's complaint against what he calls "the instability of theoretical constructs" but also with the confidence, if not arrogance, with which he opens Labov (1980: xiii). "It is often said that a field of human knowledge begins with qualitative observations and advances toward quantitative techniques as it matures." This promotion of ignorance as maturity is hard to swallow.

Let us look at statistically-oriented studies of terms of address (Brown and Gilman 1960, Brown and Ford 1961, Bates and Benigni 1975, Ervin-Tripp 1972, Friedrich 1972, Geoghegan 1970, Kess and Juricic 1978, Kramer 1975, McConnell-Ginet 1977, Mitchell 1979, Moles 1978, and Wolfson and Manes 1979). Although they vary in their statistical virtuosity, they all assume a correlational and deterministic view of meaning, a view that considers variation not subsumed by its correlational exercise as deviance. With statistical arsenals of varying degrees of sophistication, they all attempt to formulate the rules of address as *if P, then Q*, propositions where *P* refers to the set of conditions that licenses behaviour *Q*, apparently forgetting the fact that it is the interlocutors that define, sometimes as they go, the *P*'s.

The gambit of assigning humour and irony to parentheses, as in Brown and Ford (1961), or to footnotes, as in Wolfson and Manes (1979), is not even statistically fair, because humorous and sarcastic forms are not infrequent at all. But even if the normative obsession that regards humour and irony as deviation and pathology is granted to our statistically-minded investigators, they can barely cope with things like "Ah, Miss Brunet, you are like a Hollywood star tonight", said by a proud father and "*Alors, Mademoiselle, voulez-vous qu'on rentre?*", said by an affectionate mother to her sleepy 6-year old. And they must almost throw in the towel when a typically vulgar American car-salesman's enthusiastic "It was a pleasure doing business with you, Charles" elicits "It certainly was, Mr. O'Connell" from his customer.

The dilemma our statistician friend faces is beautifully summarized by Kendall (1981: 242):

> "[...] if behaviour is caused by variables, then unexpected behaviour must be caused by variables heretofore undiscovered, or alternatively, by some combination of variables heretofore uncharted ('some evidence is lacking'; 'the total number of such combinations is very high'; 'the axes would have to specify many subdivisions of the ten discriminations used above'). But if graphs of the relations between discriminations would be valid only if made for specific pairs in specific contexts, then the number of such combinations is not just 'very high', it is infinite. And if graphs of the interactions among variables are going to require 'many subdivisions' among the variables, then one might as well admit being on the route to an infinite set of ad hoc semantic discriminations."

And infinity is not the only problem. If American men use X rather than Y in the presence of older women, as Ervin-Tripp tells us, we are entitled to know how they compute "older"? In terms of chronological features alone, non-criterial properties such as ripeness, or in terms of some other mysterious variables? Given that there are enough women, even American ones, who are good at not looking their age, how, pray tell, is one to know? The statistician may know that the boundary in the population examined by him was placed at 10 years, but is the judgement that my interlocutor is about 7-8 years my senior reliable enough? I am, fortunately, not an American, but what do you do with American women who refuse to gracefully receive the deferential treatment accorded older people? There is, as the woman in the *Oil of Olay* television commercial says, "the other me". The point is that one can never know that the other person is 10 years older. The *P* in *If P, then Q* is itself subject to transactional definition.

I hope to have convinced you that the isolation of variables, the correlational and other statistical exercises that follow it, and the manipulations derived from probability theory that inform those exercises cannot in principle account either for the linguistically relevant part of variability or for mutually created social meanings that terms of address carry. Irony, humour, and sarcasm certainly fly in the face of the mild form of determinism that the metalanguage furnished by statistics invites, and the part of variability relevant for the linguist and the speaker follows from considerations well beyond that metalanguage.

Philosophically speaking, my exercise here, it seems to me, points out a problem that warrants your attention and merits serious consideration: the Platonism of mathematics. An understanding of it will also help answer the question that applied mathematicians may ask: "why should we bother with what the linguist does with statistics?" When I talk to linguists who use the metalanguage that applied mathematicians have furnished, they ask the corresponding question. Although the linguist who is tempted by mathematical metalanguage perhaps deserves harsher criticism for being scientistic, the scientist, I regret, cannot be left alone under the guise of being scientific. Besides, the fact that some mathematicians have, as I have shown, actually taken up talking about language demonstrates quite clearly their desire to universalize their special metalanguage, apparently ignoring the fact that language is produced by human beings, creatures who, within the limits imposed by biology, create and monitor their language in order to search for and impose order on the world they find themselves in, and that it is neither the black marks on a white page nor the disturbances in the air-waves, but something that can be said to be of zero dimension. Notice that I am not launching a plea for free-will, but merely saying that language is produced by actors and agents who create and interpret, and not by subjects who respond to features, variables, and probabilities. One should know the hazards of pretending to measure without changing the measured.

Where does this innocence come from? I believe it comes from what I shall call the mathematician's Platonism. Hardy (1967 [1940]) eloquently expressed that sentiment:

> "I believe that mathematical reality lies outside us, that our function is to discover or observe it, and that the theorems which we prove, and which we describe grandiloquently as our creations, are simply our notes of our observations. 317 is a prime, not because we think so, or because our minds are shaped in one way rather than another, but because it is so."

Although both his modesty *vis-à-vis* Nature and his implicit arrogance *vis-à-vis* non-mathematical observations deserve comment, I shall pass on to more pressing matters.

The fundamental problem here was first brought to our attention by Wittgenstein. He argued that Platonism presupposes precisely what it claims to explain. The smile with which the practicising mathematician expresses his joy at the poor mortal's inability to continue the sequence 2000, 2002, 2004 with anything other than 2006 does not answer the question: "what guarantees the identical character of the steps at the different stages of the application of the rule that governs the sequence?" The only guarantee there is is that mathematicians think that going from 2002 to 2004 involves precisely the same step as going from 2004 to 2006. What is conventionally consistent, in other words, is what is natural for mathematicians. With characteristically cutting clarity, Wittgenstein (1956: 155) sums up the problem of mathematical Platonism as follows: "The steps which are not brought in question are logical inferences."

Since the critique provided above calls for at least one example of what might be called the cultural relativization of mathematical entities, I am happy to provide one from Neugebauer (1952). He shows that although the Babylonians used a place-value notation, they had nothing corresponding to our use of zero when we distinguish 240 from 24. Their zero left, as Bloor (1973) puts it, some aspects of a calculation context dependent, and was, thus, very different from ours. The example shows, despite the Platonist, that concepts depend on the prevailing modes of calculation in which they enter.

Lest I should be misinterpreted as saying that there is no truth here, I should hasten to add that there is, but not of the type Hardy had in mind. The truth is, to take some liberties with Wittgenstein, that the set of conventions mathematicians and statisticians have set up has "proved to pay."

My quarrel with the use of statistical metalanguage in language-study can now be placed in its proper context. Any mathematical or statistical metalanguage is in principle incapable of describing the structure of the set of conventions we ordinary mortals internalize in the zero dimension and call our language. Although I believe that a similar case can, *mutatis mutandis*, be made for a few other human activities, I shall not attempt to do so here.

Linguistics is a search for a metalanguage that can be used to describe all natural, human languages, and inasmuch as each language may be its best metalanguage, this search may never succeed, but the possibility that statistics or mathematics may provide that metalanguage is even more remote, very, very remote indeed.

Having raised the questions of institutionality and universalisability, it is perhaps not entirely unfair to invite you to consider the possibility that the desire to use or to encourage the use of the statistical metalanguage to talk about language may in fact be the power and control side of the knowledge is power equation. The old plea that science is neutral can no longer be taken seriously, fortunately, I'd suggest. I would like to plead that one should pay some attention to the damage the use of applied mathematics tools can do to humans and their languages. Marx once said that there was no point in describing the world — one must change it. I believe he was wrong, for we change it even as we describe it. He certainly did, thus providing the best counter-example to his own theory. When you tread on my language, please be careful, partly because, as Yeats would have put it, you tread on my dreams, and partly because I guarantee that your demonstration will turn out to be redundant, irrelevant or wrong. And I mean this as *agrah*, not as *vigrah*.

Rao (1992) is, to conclude, undoubtedly right in arguing that the quantification of uncertainty has led to scientific decision making, a decision making that has paid in currencies of order and survival. I do, however, have reservations about what he calls "the ubiquity of statistics as an inevitable instrument in search of truth in all fields of inquiry". For crops, plants, migration and demographic patterns and other such things, Yes; for humans, their language, and other zero-dimension products of their minds, No. And this is so because there is no truth that is not of our making and there is no uncertainty that we do not create, negotiate, and occasionally, freeze. It may appear to be uncertainty to an outside observer, but in linguistic and human affairs, where are we to find them?

REFERENCES

Adorno, T.W. (1974). *Minima Moralia*. London: Verso.

Adorno, T.W. (1992). *Notes to Literature*. New York: Columbia University Press.

Arbib, M.A. and M.A. Hesse. (1986). *The Construction of Reality*. Cambridge: Cambridge University Press.

Auer, P. (1991). Bilingualism in/as Social Action: A Sequential Approach to Code-Switching. In H.B. Beardsmore, ed., *ESF Papers on Code Switching* vol. II. Strasbourg: ESF. 319-352.

Austin, J.L. (1956). A Plea for Excuses. In Chappell (1964). 41-63.

Backus, A. (1993). Bilingual Norms and Linguistic Change. Paper presented at *NWAVE* 22, Université d'Ottawa, Ottawa.

Bailey, C.J.B. and R. Shuy, eds. (1973). *New Ways of Analyzing Variation in English*. Washington: Georgetown University Press.

Bakker, P. (1992). *A Language of Our Own*. Amsterdam: Universiteit van Amsterdam.

Bates, E. and L. Benigni. (1975). Rules of Address in Italy: A Sociological Survey. *Language in Society* 4:3. 171-188.

Bell, R.T. (1976). *Sociolinguistics*. New York: St. Martin's Press.

Bentahila, A. and E. Davies. (1991). Constraints on Code-Switching: A Look Beyond Grammar. In *Papers for the Symposium on Code-Switching in Bilingual Studies*, Vol. 2, ESF. 369-405.

Bentahila, A. and E. Davies. (1992). Code-Switching and Language Dominance. In R.J. Harris, ed., *Cognitive Processing in Bilinguals*. Amsterdam: North Holland. 443-458.

Berk-Seligson, S. (1986). Linguistic Constraints on Intrasentential Code Switching: A Study of Spanish/Hebrew Bilingualism. *Language in Society* 15. 313-348.

Bhatia, T.K. (1989). Bilinguals' Creativity and Syntactic Theory: Evidence for Emerging Grammars. *World Englishes* 8:3. 265-276.

Bhatt, R.M. (1994). Code-Mixing and Linguistic Theory: Some Preliminary Remarks. Paper presented at the *South Asian Linguistic Analysis (SALA)* XVI Meeting, University of Pennsylvania, Philadelphia, May 20-22, 1994.

Bickerton, D. (1971). Inherent Variability and Variable Rules. *Foundations of Language* 7. 457-92.

Bloomfield, L. (1933). *Language*. New York: Henry Holt & Co.

Bloor, D. (1973). Wittgenstein and Mannheim on the Sociology of Mathematics. *Studies in the History and Philosophy of Science* 4:2. 173-191.

Boeschoten, H. (1991). Asymmetrical Code-Switching in Immigrant Communities. In H.B. Beardsmore, ed., *ESF Papers for the Workshop on Constraints, Conditions and Models*. Strasbourg: ESF.

Brainerd, B. (1974). *Weighing Evidence in Language and Literature: A Statistical Approach*. Toronto: University of Toronto Press.

Brown, R. and M. Ford. (1961). Address in American English. *Journal of Abnormal and Social Psychology* 62. 375-385.

Brown, R. and A. Gilman. (1960). The Pronouns of Power and Solidarity. In Sebeok, ed., *Style in Language*. Cambridge, Mass.: MIT Press. 253-276.

Bullokar, J. (1616). *An English Expositor*. London.

Butler, C. (1985). *Statistics in Linguistics*. Oxford: Basil Blackwell.

Cavell, C. (1958). Must We Mean What We Say? In Chappell (1964). 75-112.

Cawdrey, R. (1604). *A Table Alphabeticall*. London.

Chappell, V.C., ed. (1964). *Ordinary Language*. New York: Dover.

Chick, J.K. (1985). The Interactional Accomplishment of Discrimination in South Africa. *Language in Society* 14. 299-326.

Chomsky, N. (1963). Formal Properties of Grammars. In R. Luce, R.

Bush and E. Gallanter, eds., *Handbook of Mathematical Psychology* 2. New York: John Wiley.

Chomsky, N. (1980). *Rules and Representations*. New York: Columbia.

Chomsky, N. (1985). *The Knowledge and Use of Language*. New York: Praeger.

Chomsky, N. (1987). *On Power and Ideology*. Boston: South End Press.

Chomsky, N. (1988). *Language and Problems of Knowledge*. Cambridge, Mass.: MIT Press.

Clyne, M. (1991). Concluding Remarks. In H.B. Beardsmore, ed., *ESF Papers on Code-Switching*. Strasbourg: ESF.

Cockeram, H. (1623). *The English Dictionarie: Or an Interpreter of Hard English Words*. London.

D'Souza, J. (1992). Varieties of English Old and New: A Matter of Standards. Unpublished MS. The National University of Singapore.

Dasgupta, P. (1993). *The Otherness of English*. Delhi: Sage.

DeCamp, D. (1971). Towards a Generative Analysis of a Post-Creole Speech Continuum. In D. Hymes, ed., *Pidginization and Creolization of Languages*. Cambridge: Cambridge University Press. 349-370.

DiSciullo, A.-M., P. Muysken and R. Singh. (1986). Government and Code Mixing. *Journal of Linguistics* 22:1. 1-24.

Drapeau, L. (forthcoming). Code-Switching in Caretaker Speech and Bilingual Competence in a Native Village of Northern Quebec. *IJSL.*

Durkheim, E. (1938). *The Rules of Sociological Method*. New York: Free Press.

Eliasson, S. (1990). English-Maori Language Contact. In R. Filipovic and M.Bratanic, eds.., *Languages in Contact: Proceedings of the Symposium 16.1 of the 12th International Congress of Anthropological and Ethnological Sciences*. Zagreb: Institute of Linguistics, University of Zagreb. 33-49.

Eliasson, S. (1991). Models and Constraints in Code-Switching Theory. In *Papers for the ESF Workshop on Constraints, Conditions, and Models*. Strasbourg: ESF. 17-50.

Elliot, T.S. (1942). *Four Quartets*. London: Faber.

Emeneau, M.B. (1956). India as a Linguistic Area. *Language* 32:1. 3-16.

Ervin-Tripp, S. (1972). On So-called Rules: Alternation and Co-occurrence. In J. Gumperz and D. Hymes, eds., *Directions in Sociolinguistics*. New-York: Holt, Rinehart & Winston. 300-324.

Fasold. R.W. (1991). The Quiet Demise of Variable Rules. *American Speech* 66:1. 3-21.

Felix, S. (1988) Universal Grammar in Language Acquisition. *The Canadian Journal of Linguistics* 33:4. 345-366.

Ferguson, C. and J.J. Gumperz. (1960). *Linguistic Diversity in South Asia. Indiana University Research Center in Anthropology, Folklore and Linguistics Publications 13*. Bloomington, Ind.: Indiana University Press.

Fishman, J. (1972). *The Sociology of Language*. Rowley: Newbury.

Fishman, J. (1992). Foreword to G. Williams, *Sociolinguistics: A Sociological Critique*. London: Routledge. vii-ix.

Foucault, M. (1969). La grammaire générale de Port-Royal. *Langages* 7.

Foucault, M. (1980). *Power-Knowledge*. Brighton: Harvester.

Friedrich, P. (1972). Social Context and Semantic Feature: The Russian Pronominal Usage. In Gumperz and Hymes. 273-300.

Gadamer, H.G. (1981). *Reason in the Age of Science*. Cambridge, Mass.: MIT Press.

Geoghegan, W. (1970). A Theory of Marking Rules. *Working Paper* 37. Language Behaviour Research Laboratory. Berkeley.

Giesbers, H. (1989). *Code Switching Tussen Dialect en Standaardtaal*. Amsterdam: P.J. Meertens Institut voor Dialectologie.

Goffman, E. (1964). The Neglected Situation. *American Anthropologist* 66:6/2. 133-6.

Grosjean, F. (1982). *Life With Two Languages*. Cambridge, Mass.: Harvard University Press.

Grosjean, F. (1991). Comments on Hyltenstam. *Papers for the ESF Workshop on Constraints, Conditions, and Models*. Strasbourg: ESF. 255-258.

Grosjean, F. (in press). The On-Line Processing of Speech: Lexical Access in Bilinguals. In Bhatt and Davies, eds., *The Bilingual Brain*. Toronto: C.U.P.

Gumperz, J.J. (1971). *Language in Social Groups*. Stanford: Stanford University Press.

Gumperz, J.J. (1976). The Socio-Linguistic Significance of Conversational Code-Switching. In Gumperz and Gumperz, eds., *Papers on Language and Context*. *Working Paper* 46. Language Behaviour Research Laboratory. Berkeley: University of California. 1-46.

Gumperz, J.J. (1982a). *Discourse Strategies*. Cambridge: Cambridge University Press.

Gumperz, J.J., ed. (1982b). *Language and Social Identity*. Cambridge: Cambridge University Press.

Gupta, D. (1980). From *Varna* to *Jati*: The Indian Caste System from Asiatic Mode of Production to Feudalism. *Journal of Contemporary Asia* 10:3. 299-399.

Guy, G. (1980). Variation in the Group and the Individual: The Case of Final Stop Deletion. In Labov, ed., *Language in Space and Time*. New York: Academic Press. 1-36.

Habermas, J. (1976). Toward a theory of Communicative Competence. In H.P. Dreitzel, ed., *Recent Sociology*. London: MacMillan. 114-48.

Habermas, J. (1977). A Review of Gadamer's *Truth and Method*. In F. Dallmayrand and T. McCarthy, eds., *Understanding and Social Inquiry*. Notre Dame, Ind.: University of Notre Dame Press. 335-63.

Habermas, J. (1979). *Communication and the Evolution of Society*, Boston: Beacon Press.

Habermas, J. (1984). *The Theory of Communicative Action*, Boston: Beacon Press.

Habermas, J. (1987). *The Philosophical Discourse of Modernity*. Cambridge, Mass.: MIT Press.

Hakuta, K. (1984). In What Ways Are Language Universals Psychologically Real? In W. Rutherford, ed., *Language Universals and Second Language Acquisition*. Amsterdam: Benjamins. 223-238.

Halliday, M.A.K. (1975). *Learning How to Mean: Explorations in the Development of Language*. London: Edward Arnold.

Hansen-Bhatt, B. and R. Bhatt (1992). On the Nature of L1 Filter and Cross-Language Transfer Effects. Paper presented at *New Sounds 92*, University of Amsterdam, April 1992.

Hardy, G.H. (1967 [1940]). *A Mathematician's Apology*. Cambridge: Cambridge University Press.

Harris, J. (1984). Syntactic Variation and Dialect Divergence. *Journal of Linguistics* 20. 303-327.

Hatch, E. and H. Farhady. (1982). *Research Design and Statistics for Applied Linguistics*. Cambridge, Mass.: Newbury House.

Haugen, E. (1953). *The Norwegian Language in America*. Philadelphia: University of Pennsylvania Press.

Hickey R. (1983). Syntactic Ambiguity in Hiberno-English. *Studia Anglica Posnaniensia* 15. 39-46.

Hock, H. and R. Pandharipande. (1978). Sanskrit in the Pre-Islamic Sociolinguistic Context of South Asia. *International Journal of the Sociology of Language* 1. 11-25.

Hyltenstam, K. (1990). Language Mixing in Alzheimer's Dementia. *ESF Papers for the ESF Workshop on Constraints, Conditions, and Models*. Strasbourg: ESF. 27-39.

Hymes, D. (1983). Report from an Under-developed Country: Toward Linguistic Competence in the United States. In B. Bain, ed., *The Sociogenesis of Language and Human Conduct*. New York: Plenum. 189-224.

Jackendoff, R. (1983). *Semantics and Cognition*. Cambridge, Mass.: MIT Press.

Jones, R.H. (1975). Probability Estimation Using a Multinomial Logistic Function. *Journal of Statistical Computation and Simulation* 3. 315-329.

Joos, M. (1942). A Phonological Dilemma in Canadian English. *Language* 18. 141-144.

Joshi, A. (1985). Processing of Sentences with Intrasentential Code-Switching. In D. Dowty, L. Kartunen and A. Zwicky, eds., *Natural Language Parsing: Psychological, Computational and Theoretical Perspectives*. Cambridge: Cambridge University Press. 190-205.

Kachru, B. (1976). Indian English: A Sociolinguistic Profile of a Transplanted Language. *Studies in Language Learning* 1:2.

Kachru, B. (1978). Toward Structuring Code-mixing: An Indian Perspective. *IJSL* 16. 27-46.

Kachru, B. (1980). Socially Realistic Linguistics: The Firthian Tradition. *Studies in the Linguistic Sciences* 10:1. 85-112. University of Illinois, Urbana.

Kant, I. (1966 [1781]). *Critique of Pure Reason*. Tr. by Max Müller. Garden City, N.Y.: Doubleday Anchor.

Kaplan, R. (1966). Cultural Thought Patterns in Intercultural Education. *Language Learning* 16. 1-20.

Kendall, M.B. (1981). Toward a Semantic Approach to Terms of Address: A Critique of Deterministic Models in Sociolinguistics. *Language and Communication* 1:2/3. 237-254.

Kersey, J. (1702). *A New English Dictionary*. London.

Kess, J.F. and Z.B. Juricic. (1978). Slovene Pronominal Address Forms: Rural vs Urban Sociolinguistic Strategies. *Anthropological Linguistics* 20:7. 297-311.

Kiparsky, P. (1988). Phonological Change. In F. Newmeyer, ed., *The Cambridge Survey of Linguistics*. Cambridge: Cambridge University Press.

Kramer, C. (1975). Sex-related Differences in Address Systems. *Anthropological Linguistics* 17:5. 198-210.

Labov, W. (1970). The Study of Language in Its Social Context. *Studium Generale* 23. 30-87.

Labov, W. (1971). Methodology. In W.O. Dingwall, ed., *A Survey of Linguistic Science*. College Park: Univ. of Maryland. 419-497.

Labov, W. (1980). *Locating Language in Time and Space*. New York: Academic Press.

Labov, W. (1987). The Interpretation of Zeroes. In Dressler *et al*, eds., *Phonologica 1984*. Cambridge: Cambridge University Press. 135-156.

Lakoff, R. (1973). Language and Woman's Place. *Language in Society* 2. 45-80.

Lass, R. (1986). Irish Influence: Reflections on Standard English and its Opposites,. *Studia Anglica Posnaniensia* 18. 81-88.

Lavandera, B.R. (1978). Where Does the Sociolinguistic Variable Stop? *Language in Society* 7. 171-182.

Lele, J.K. and R. Singh. (1989). *Language and Society: Steps Towards an Integrated Theory*. Leiden: E.J. Brill.

Lindsey, J.K. (1975). Likelihood Analyses and Tests for Binary Data. *Applied Statistics* 24. 1-16.

Maltz, D. and R.A. Borker. (1982). A Cultural Approach to Male-Female Miscommunication. In Gumperz (1982b). 195-216.

Martinet, A. (1953). Preface to Weinreich (1953). vii-ix.

Martinet, A. (1984). On Morphophonology. Paper presented at Phonologica 1984. Eisenstadt, Austria.

Mates, B. (1958). On the Verification of Statements about Ordinary Language. In Chappell (1964). 64-74.

McArthur, T. (1986). The Power of Words: Pressure, Prejudice and Politics in Our Vocabularies and Dictionaries. *World Englishes* 5:2. 209-219.

McCarthy, T. (1978). *The Critical Theory of Jürgen Habermas*. Cambridge, Mass.: MIT Press.

McConnell-Ginet, S. (1977). Address Forms and Sexual Politics. Paper presented at the 1977 *CUNY* Conference on Language and Style.

Mey, J. L. (1985) *Whose Language?* Amsterdam: Benjamins.

Mitchell, S. (1979). Address and Decision Making in Modern Swedish. *Anthropological Linguistics* 21:2. 61-69.

Mohanan, K.P. (1992). Describing the Phonology of Non-native Varieties of a Language. *World Englishes* 11:2. 111-128.

Moles, J. (1978). Decision and Variability. *Anthropological Linguistics* 21:2. 61-69.

Myers-Scotton, C. (1990). Intersections between Social Motivations and Structural Processing in Code-Switching. *ESF Papers on Code-Switching*. Strasbourg: ESF. 57-82.

Nadkarni, M. (1975). Bilingualism and Syntactic Change in Konkani. *Language* 51. 672-683.

Neugebauer, O. (1952). *The Exact Sciences in Antiquity*. Princeton, N.J.: Princeton University Press.

Nortier, J. (1990). *Dutch-Moroccan Code-Switching*. Dordrecht: Foris.

Nortier, J. (1991). Dutch-Moroccan Arabic Code-Switching in the Netherlands. *Papers for the Symposium on Code-Switching in Bilingual Studies: Theory, Significance and Perspectives*. Strasbourg: ESF. 517-522.

Omvedt, G. (1985). Development of the Caste System in South Asia: Notes Towards a Theory. *In the Wake of Marx* 1:4. 3-18.

Pakir, A. (1991). The Range and Depth of English-Knowing Bilinguals in Singapore. *World Englishes* 10:2. 167-179.

Pandharipande, R. (1981). On the Nativization of Lexicon: The Case of Marathi. *Linguistics* 19:9/10. 987-1007.

Pandharipande, R. (1986). Language Contact and Language Variation: Nagpuri Marathi. In B. KrishnamurthI *et al*, eds., *South Asian Languages: Structure, Convergence and Diglossia*. Delhi: Motilal Banarsidas. 219-231.

Pandit, I. (1986). *Hindi-English Code Switching, Mixed Hindi-English*. Delhi: Datta Book Centre.

Pfaff, C. (1976). Code-Switching and Syntactic Change. In S.B. Steever *et al*, eds., *Papers from the Parasession on Diachronic Syntax*. Chicago: Chicago Linguistic Society. 248-259.

Pfaff, C. (1979). Constraints on Language-Mixing: Intrasentential Code-switching and Borrowing in Spanish/English. *Language* 55. 291-318.

Poplack, S. (1980). Sometimes I'll Start a Sentence in English y Termino en Español. *Linguistics* 18. 581-618.

Popper, K. and J. Eccles. (1977). *The Self and Its Brain*. London.

Postal, P. (1969). On So-called "Pronouns" in English. In D.A. Reibel and S.A. Schane, eds., *Modern Studies in English*. Englewood Cliffs, N.J.: Prentice-Hall. 201-224.

Prabhu, N.S. (1989). The Mathetic Function of English as a World Language. Paper presented at the TESL Conference, Islamabad, Pakistan, January 1989.

Quirk, R. (1991). Language Varieties and Standard Language. In M.L. Tickoo, ed., *Language and Standards: Issues, Attitudes, Case Studies*. Singapore: Seameo. 165-177.

Rai, A. (1986). *A House Divided*. Delhi: Oxford University Press.

Rao, C.R. (1992). *Statistics and Truth: Putting Chance to Work*. Bartonsville, Maryland: International Cooperative Publishing House.

Rousseau, P. (1989). A Versatile Program for the Analysis of Sociolinguistic Data. In R.W. Fasold and D. Schiffrin, eds., *Language Change and Variation*. Amsterdam: Benjamins. 395-410.

Rousseau, P. and D. Sankoff. (1978). Advances in Variable Rule Methodology. In D. Sankoff (1978). 57-70.

Sahgal, M. (1991). Patterns of Language Use in a Bilingual Setting in India. In J. Cheshire, ed., *English Around the World*. Cambridge: Cambridge University Press. 299-306.

Sankoff, D. (1978). *Linguistic Variation: Models and Methods*. New York: Academic Press.

Sankoff, D. and S. Poplack. (1981). A Formal Grammar for Code-Switching. *Papers in Linguistics* 14. 13-46.

Shapiro, M.C. and H.F. Schiffman. (1981). *Language and Society in South Asia*. Delhi: Motilal Banarasidas.

Singh, R. (1980). In Defense of the Universal Syllabic Template. Paper presented at the 1980 annual meeting of the CLA/ACL. Montréal.

Singh, R. (1981). Grammatical Constraints on Code Mixing. *Recherches Linguistiques à Montréal* 17. 155-163.

Singh, R. (1982). On Some Redundant Compounds in Modern Hindi. *Lingua* 56. 345-351.

Singh, R. (1983). We, They, and Us: A Note on Code-Switching and Social Stratification in North-India. *Language in Society* 12. 71-73.

Singh, R. (1984). Explorations in the Ethnography of Discourse. In V.S. Penkadur, ed., *South Asian Horizons* 2. Vancouver: University of British Columbia.

Singh, R. (1985a). Formal and Social Aspects of Language Contact. *ITL* 70. 33-60

Singh, R. (1985b). Grammatical Constraints on Code-Switching: Evidence from Hindi/English. *Canadian Journal of Linguistics*. 30. 33-45.

Singh, R. (1986). Linguistic Theory and Language Contact. Report to the Social Sciences and Humanities Research Council of Canada. Mimeo. Université de Montréal.

Singh, R. (1987). On the Redundant Nature of Variable Rules. *ALH* 20. 111-17.

Singh, R. (1994). Indian English: Some Conceptual Issues. In R.K. Agnihotri and A.L. Khanna, eds., *Second Language Acquisition*, Thousand Oaks: Sage. 369-381.

Singh, R., ed. (1996a). *Towards a Critical Sociolinguistics*. Amsterdam: Benjamins.

Singh, R. (1996b). A Natural Phono(morpho)logy: A View from the Outside. In B. Hurch and R.D. Rhodes, eds., *Natural Phonology: The State of the Art*. Berlin: Mouton. 1-38.

Singh, R. (forthcoming). Hindi-English Code-Mixing: Some Implications for a General Theory. *Indian Linguistics*. (Revised version of the paper presented at Max Planck, 1992).

Singh, R. and A. Ford. (1988). A Closer Look at So-called Variable Processes. In R.W. Fasold and D. Schiffrin, eds. *Language Change and Variation*. Amsterdam: Benjamins. 360-380.

Singh, R. and M. Kully. (1982). Nativization and German *-IEREN*. *The Canadian Journal of Linguistics* 27:1. 55-58.

Singh, R. and J.K. Lele. (1985). Remarks on Marathi and Language Contact. In P.H. Nelde, ed., *Methoden der KontaktLinguistik*. Bonn: Dummler. 269-95.

Singh, R. and J.K. Lele. (1987). Conversations with a Door-Mat: Language, Power and Cross-Sex Communication Strategies. *Economic and Political Weekly* July 4. 1093-94.

Singh, R., J.K. Lele and G. Martohardjono. (1988). Communication in a Multilingual Society: Some Missed Opportunities. *Language in Society* 17. 43-59.

Singh, R. *et al.* (1995). On 'New/Non-Native' Englishes. *Journal of Pragmatics* 24:3. 283-294.

Stratford, P. (1992). *The Rage of Space*. Montreal: Oberon..

Terrell, T. (1977). Universal Constraints on Variably Deleted Consonants: Evidence from Spanish. *Canadian Journal of Linguistics* 22. 156-168.

Tiersma, P.M. (1982). Local and General Markedness. *Language* 58. 832-848.

Todd, L. (1986). *Pidgins and Creoles*. London: Longmans.

Tosi, A. (1991). First, Second, or Foreign Language Learning. In H. B. Beadsmore, ed., *ESF Papers on Code-Switching*. Strasbourg: ESF. 353-368.

Tranel, B. (1976). A Note on Final Consonant Deletion in Modern French. *Lingua* 39. 53-68.

Valentine, T. (1985). Sex, Power, and Linguistic Strategies in the Hindi Language. *Studies in the Linguistic Sciences* 15:1. 195-211.

Valentine, T. (1986). Language and Power: Cross-Sex Communicative Strategies in Hindi and Indian English. *Economic and Political Weekly* (Special Issue: *Review of Women Studies*) 21:43. 75-87.

Varonis, E.M. and S. Gass. (1985). Miscommunication in Native/Non-native Conversation. *Language in Society* 14. 327-343.

Weinreich, U. (1953). *Languages in Contact*. The Hague: Mouton.

West, C. and D.H. Zimmerman. (1983). Small Insults: A Study of Interruptions in Cross-Sex Conversations between Unacquainted Persons. In B. Thorne *et al*, eds., *Language, Gender, and Sex*. Rowley, Mass.: Newbury House. 102-117.

Wittgenstein, L. (1956). *Remarks on the Foundations of Mathematics*. Oxford: Blackwell.

Wolfram, W. (1974). *Sociolinguistic Aspects of Assimilation*. Arlington, Va.: Center for Applied Linguistics.

Wolfson, N. and J. Manes. (1979). Don't Dear Me! *Working Papers in Sociolinguistics* 53.

Zimmerman, D.H., and C. West (1975). Sex Roles, Interruptions, and Silences in Conversation. In B. Thorne and N. Henley, eds., *Language and Sex: Difference and Dominance*. Rowley, Mass.: Newbury House. 105-129.

INDEX OF NAMES AND LANGUAGES